S0-BIQ-979

THE FLANNERY TWO DIAMOND OPENING

by Bill Flannery

Published by
Devyn Press
Louisville, Kentucky

Cover by Bonnie Baron Pollack

Copyright © 1984 by Devyn Press

All rights reserved. No part of this
book may be reproduced in any form
without the permission of Devyn Press.

Printed in the United States of America.
Devyn Press
151 Thierman Lane
Louisville, KY 40207

ISBN 0-910791-13-9

DEDICATION

This book is dedicated to my wife, Marlene, and our four children, Bill, Patrick, Kimberly and Darrell.

ACKNOWLEDGMENT

I am deeply indebted to Richard A. Finberg, of Pittsburgh, a keen analyst and writer of many bridge articles. He spent much time on the development of this book, and without his effort and cooperation every step of the way, my favorite convention would not have been so explicitly and accurately presented.

TABLE OF CONTENTS

MISADVENTURES WITH FLANNERY

It all began innocently enough when my partner Shirley asked, "David, why don't we play Flannery tonight?"

"Sure," I answered. After all, I did know the convention — with five hearts and four spades and between 11 and 16 points, you open 2 ◊.

Soon thereafter, I did just that, and partner bid 2 NT. Hmm, I thought, I've described my hand . . . if partner wants to play it there, let her . . . she must know what she's doing.

After the hand went down, Shirley suggested, "David, why don't we not play Flannery?"

"Okay," I said. "I don't much like Flannery anyway."

"There's more to Flannery than just bidding 2 ◊," she answered.

"Oh," I muttered.

Several years later, my friend Sam explained the rest of the convention to me. He finished by telling me that 2 ◊ wasn't Flannery, 2 ♡ was. 2 ◊ was something else. I vetoed that notion and began to play Flannery again.

How proud I was when first I bid Flannery knowingly. I stood on the chair and announced "Two Diamonds!" From that point on, the bidding went downhill, and we would end up playing in 1 ♣ (just kidding, but the bidding was bad). After several rounds of bidding, we arrived at our final contract. How proud my right hand opponent was when she knowingly stood on her chair and announced, "Double!" After several other bad results, we discarded Flannery.

But not playing Flannery with Sam was worse than playing it. During one session, he kept getting five hearts and four spades in his hand so often that it frustrated him. With no collusion on our part, he decided to open Flannery hands 1 ♣. After the second time, I started to alert all 1 ♣ bids as "possible Flannery."

Theresa came next. Not only were we playing Flannery, but also a lot of other conventions that I couldn't remember. They never came up — at least I don't think so. One night Theresa opened 2◊. I was about to alert "Flannery" when I glanced at the convention card, and Flannery wasn't there. I called "Pause" and tried to remember when we had discarded Flannery (most of my partners wouldn't let me play Flannery and some other conventions with which we had had problems). I couldn't remember one way or the other, but since convention cards don't lie, I passed. We were cold for 4♡, or was it 6♡? It was easier to explain that I had forgotten and secretly added Flannery to our convention card later.

The most recent misadventure occurred with Judy. You see, I had this weak two diamond bid. Judy alerted and bid, "Two notrump." I gulped, and it went pass, pass by me, glare by Judy (out of turn), pass.

"Sorry," I said to Judy, "I thought we were playing Flimflannery."

But that wasn't the end of the story. I made the mistake of putting my six card diamond suit where trumps belong and distraught Judy thought we were playing some number of diamonds. So, she took all her winners, led a small losing card and said, "Hit it!"

"What do you mean, 'hit it'?" I replied, as they took the balance of the tricks. Flannery is fun, eh?

I've been playing Flannery on and off again for seven years and have yet to bid one to an appropriate conclusion. Recently, though, I may have met someone with whom I can play Flannery. At a small stakes rubber bridge game, I suggested to partner Joel that we play Flannery. He hesitantly said, "Yes," but added that he didn't know the convention very well.

"I think we'll get along just fine," I smiled.

A little knowledge only goes a little way. What could be better than learning from Flannery himself how to play his convention correctly? This book tells you everything you will ever need to know about the Flannery convention. Many ideas in this book are useful as well in auctions not involving Flannery — such as when to choose a 4-3 trump fit in preference to a 5-2 trump fit and when not to make a transfer bid.

I like to think that this book is dedicated to me and all other players who have from time to time encountered a question about a Flannery auction and wondered what Flannery would have done. Now, we will know.

David Hutchinson

Author's note:
Dave Hutchinson is well known in the Philadelphia, Pennsylvania, area for his humorous contributions to bridge publications.

WHY FLANNERY?

Why a whole book on one convention? Since Flannery hands come up frequently, they are a very important class of hands. Because you hold the majors and an opening bid, your side will usually play the contract. Also, some important improvements have been made since the convention was accepted in 1965. Most noteworthy are the 3♣ response to 2◇ (which is now natural); the new conventional 3◇ response (which is used to locate top honors in spades and hearts); the reason for responding 3♡ or 3♠ instead of 2 NT on certain types of hands; and competitive sequences designed to preserve the accuracy of the Flannery system and to offer maximum opportunity to double opponents. In addition, a defensive structure is suggested for competing against Flannery.

The four main reasons for using Flannery:
1. It describes major suit holdings with an opening bid and a hand not good enough to reverse.
2. It forces the opponents to compete at a higher level and makes it difficult for them to evaluate their hands.
3. It enables responder to evaluate his hand according to his major suit holdings.
4. The 2 NT response, the best response in the system, enables responder to get a complete picture of opener's hand and to place the hand at the proper contract.

The Flannery 2◇ opening solves the awkward bidding problem that occurs when opener has four spades and five hearts without enough strength to reverse. If opener bids 1♠, and then hearts, responder will think opener has equal or greater length in spades. If opener bids 1♡, he will be unable to bid spades after a two-level response without exaggerating his strength. If the partnership is playing the forcing notrump response to one of a major, the problem is especially severe when opener has 4-5-2-2 distribution, since after opening 1♡ and hearing partner respond 1 NT, opener cannot rebid 2♡ without six hearts, and cannot rebid two of a minor with only two cards in the suit.

While solving this four spade-five heart dilemma, the Flannery convention proves easy to handle and highly effective. 2◊ has little practical use for other bids. The "weak two bid" in diamonds virtually invites the opponents to compete in two of a major, and, if the weak two bidder has three card support for a major, he risks losing the best fit. Moreover, 3◊ can be bid on most hands suitable for a weak two diamond bid. Expert partnerships who wish to reserve 2◊ for some other meaning, such as Roman (showing strong hands with 4-4-4-1 or 5-4-4-0 distribution with shortage in any suit), can also use Flannery by substituting 2♡ for the opening bid.

Chapter I

The Opening Flannery 2◊ Bid

Chapter I

The Opening Flannery 2 ◊ Bid

Any hand containing exactly four spades, five hearts and 11 to 16 high card points (HCP) is a probable Flannery opening bid. The only exceptions occur at the extremes. Hands containing only 11 or 12 HCP with little strength in the long suits or lacking quick tricks should be passed in first and second seat. At the other end of the spectrum, some 16 HCP hands are too good.

In evaluating your hand as opener, do not count distributional points. Responder will add distributional points to his hand if a good major suit fit is found. Naturally, hands with 3-1 or 4-0 distribution in the minor suits are preferred to hands with doubletons in both minors. Nevertheless, as you will see, responder will be able to determine your exact distribution. Your short suits may or may not be of value to partner, who can decide for himself. Therefore, it is best to ignore distributional points.

Flannery uses standard high card point evaluation (Ace = 4, King = 3, Queen = 2, and Jack = 1). In addition, three other factors are considered:
1. Quick tricks
2. Suit quality
3. To the limited extent mentioned above, distribution.

These factors are discussed next.

Evaluating Your Hand[1]

(1) Quick Tricks

"Quick tricks" are an estimate of how many tricks your hand is likely to win in the first two rounds that a suit is played. The following is a table of quick tricks:

AK $= 2$
AQ $= 1\frac{1}{2}$
A $\;\; = 1$
KQ $= 1$
Kx $= \frac{1}{2}$
K $\;\; = 0$

Quick tricks are desirable both offensively and defensively as they provide control of the hand. They enable you to interrupt your opponent's plan of attack to pursue your own battle campaign. Hands rich in quick tricks generally have better game and slam potential than hands with less quick tricks but the same HCP. And, they generally offer better defensive prospects.

Quick tricks are not an infallible guide. Note, for example, that Axx and KQx both count as one quick trick. The trick representing the ace is considerably more secure and can be taken sooner. On the other hand, the KQx may ultimately provide two tricks, not one.

Hands rich in quick tricks should be viewed favorably when making close decisions such as whether to open the bidding or accept a game invitation.

(2) Suit Quality

Hands with honor cards in the long suits are much stronger than hands with their strength concentrated in the

[1]Experienced players may wish to skip to page 15. The hand evaluation principles discussed here apply to all bidding, not just Flannery auctions.

short suits. Close decisions in deciding whether to open or to accept game or slam invitations should be strongly influenced by the location of the high cards. Compare the two hands below:

(a) ♠ A J x x   (b) ♠ K x x x
     ♡ K Q J x x   ♡ J x x x x
     ◊ x x x   ◊ A J x
     ♣ x   ♣ Q

Hand (a) qualifies for a Flannery opening. Hand (b) does not. Both contain the same high cards.

In the hands above, the quick trick count leads to the same conclusion. Hand (a) contains 2 quick tricks, while hand (b) contains only 1½ quick tricks. Even if the quick trick count and number of HCP are identical, concentration of strength in long suits is desirable. For example:

(c) ♠ A J 10 x   (d) ♠ J 10 x x
     ♡ A J 9 x x   ♡ J 9 x x x
     ◊ J x x   ◊ A J x
     ♣ x   ♣ A

Hand (c) should be opened. Hand (d) should not be opened, despite identical high card strength, except in third and fourth seat.

Another aspect of suit quality is the "body" of the suits, that is, whether they contain 10's, 9's, and 8's. Strict obedience to HCP does not account for spot cards. You must make this adjustment yourself. Which hand of the following two do you prefer?

(e) ♠ A Q 10 2   (f) ♠ A Q 4 2
     ♡ K Q 10 9 7   ♡ K Q 9 3 2
     ◊ J 10 2   ◊ J 6 2
     ♣ 2   ♣ 8

Could the choice be any easier? In both cases, the HCP and quick tricks are identical. In both cases, the honors head long suits. Nevertheless, hand (e) is clearly better than hand (f) because of its better spot cards. The heart suit in hand (e) is likely to produce three tricks even if partner has a small singleton. In hand (f), the heart suit seldom produces three tricks opposite a small singleton.

(3) Distribution

Hands with 4-5-3-1, 4-5-1-3, 4-5-4-0 or 4-5-0-4 distribution are clearly better, on the average, than hands with 4-5-2-2 distribution, since your trumps can nullify high cards held by your opponents in the short suit. Accordingly, hands containing a singleton or void are to be preferred, and in borderline cases, this consideration is given some weight. In a similar vein, a 16 HCP hand is more likely to be too strong for a Flannery opening if it contains a singleton or void. (See page 18, "Hands Too Strong for Flannery").

It is to be emphasized, however, that on most constructive auctions, responder will ascertain your exact distribution through use of the 2 NT response. Responder will know whether the hands fit well and will take that into account in his bidding. Accordingly, in those situations, opener should give no further weight to his minor suit shape in evaluating his hand.

Minimum Flannery Openings

Hands containing only 11 HCP should ordinarily not be opened unless they contain 2½ quick tricks or exceptional suit quality. Hands with 12 HCP should usually have at least 2 quick tricks, depending on suit quality. All hands with 13 HCP should be opened. These rules are not rigid. Some 11 to 12 HCP hands with only 1½ quick tricks qualify for an opening Flannery bid if the major suits are very strong. The following are some dead minimum opening bids. They do not meet the above recommendations but have strong majors:

1. ♠ A Q J x
   ♡ Q J 10 x x   (12 HCP; 1½ quick tricks)
   ◇ Q x x
   ♣ x

2. ♠ K Q 10 x
   ♡ K J 10 9 x   (11 HCP; 1½ quick tricks)
   ◇ Q x x
   ♣ x

3. ♠ K J 10 x
   ♡ K Q J 10 x   (11 HCP; 1½ quick tricks)
   ◇ J x x
   ♣ x

4. ♠ Q J 9 x
   ♡ A Q J x x   (11 HCP; 1½ quick tricks)
   ◇ x
   ♣ J x x

5. ♠ Q 10 9 x
   ♡ A Q J x x   (11 HCP; 1½ quick tricks)
   ◇ x
   ♣ Q 10 x

6. ♠ K Q 10 x
   ♡ Q J 10 x x   (11 HCP; 1½ quick tricks)
   ◇ K x x
   ♣ x

16

If you have been weaned on Goren's Point Count, you may find the above examples too aggressive for your taste. Bear in mind, however, that on Flannery hands you control the major suits, and in the above examples, the suits are strong. Also, since Flannery is a highly descriptive bid, it is best to use it whenever possible. Should the opponents set up a barrage of preemptive bids in clubs or diamonds after you open, partner will be in an excellent position to place the final contract.

The following are examples of minimum range Flannery opening bids which are somewhat richer in quick tricks:

7. ♠ A K x x
   ♡ K J x x x   (11 HCP; 2½ quick tricks)
   ◊ x x x
   ♣ x

8. ♠ K Q 9 x
   ♡ K Q 10 9 x   (12 HCP; 2 quick tricks)
   ◊ Q x x
   ♣ x

In summary, the following is a useful guide for determining whether you have sufficient strength to open Flannery:

    11 HCP with 2½ quick tricks
    12 HCP with 2 quick tricks
    Any 13 HCP hand

These requirements may be relaxed when the major suits are very strong.

Third and Fourth Seat Openings

In third or fourth seat, you may shade the requirements for Flannery just as you would any other opening bid. Because the Flannery bid is so descriptive, I recommend that you open 2♢ on any hand with four spades and five hearts that you would otherwise open light in third seat. Partner, whose hand is limited, must allow for the possibility that you have opened light and should press on to game only with a maximum hand and a very good fit for one or more of your suits.

Hands Too Strong for Flannery

Your hand is too strong for Flannery if it justifies a reverse, that is, a 1♡ opening followed by a 2♠ rebid. Hands containing 17 HCP are too strong to open 2♢. Hands with 16 HCP are borderline. Suit quality, quick tricks, and distribution should be considered.

The following hands are slightly too good to open Flannery:

9. ♠ A Q J x
   ♡ K Q J 10 x
   ♢ A x x (17 HCP)
   ♣ x

10. ♠ A Q 10 x
    ♡ A K 10 9 x
    ♢ x   (16 HCP)
    ♣ K 10 x

11. ♠ A J 10 x
    ♡ K Q J x x
    ♢ K x (17 HCP)
    ♣ K x

12. ♠ K J 10 x
    ♡ A K J 10 x
    ♢ A x x (16 HCP)
    ♣ x

None of these hands are good enough to insist on game after a simple response by partner. In all the above examples, I would insist on game after a heart raise or a

1♠ response. Each hand has at least 19 supporting points for the majors. (When not opening Flannery, distributional points must be added when raising partner's suit).

In each of the above examples, I would bid 2♠ after a 1 NT, 2♣ or 2♢ response by partner. This is game forcing after the 2♣ or 2♢ response (which shows at least ten points regardless of system). After the 1 NT response by partner, I play that a 2♠ reverse is not forcing.

QUIZ

Chapter I
Opening Flannery Bids

State whether these hands should be opened Flannery 2♦, assuming you are in first or second seat.

1. ♠ A Q x x
   ♡ K x x x x
   ◇ K x x
   ♣ x

2. ♠ K Q x x x
   ♡ A J x x
   ◇ A x
   ♣ x x

3. ♠ Q x x x
   ♡ K Q x x x x
   ◇ x
   ♣ A K

4. ♠ x x x x
   ♡ x x x x x
   ◇ A K
   ♣ K x

5. ♠ x x x x
   ♡ x x x x x
   ◇ A K
   ♣ A x

6. ♠ J x x x
   ♡ A K Q 10 x
   ◇ A x x
   ♣ x

7. ♠ A K Q J
   ♡ x x x x x
   ◇ K x x
   ♣ x

8. ♠ A Q 10 9
   ♡ Q J 9 x x
   ◇ Q x
   ♣ J x

9. ♠ A K 10 x
   ♡ A Q J 10 x
   ◇ Q x
   ♣ x x

10. ♠ A J 10 x
    ♡ A K 10 x x
    ◇ K J x
    ♣ x

11. ♠ K Q 9 x
    ♡ Q J 10 x x
    ◇ Q x x
    ♣ Q

12. ♠ K Q 10 x
    ♡ K Q J 10 9
    ◇ A x x
    ♣ x

ANSWERS TO CHAPTER I QUIZ

1. Yes. 12 HCP; 2½ quick tricks.
2. No. This hand has five spades and four hearts. Don't confuse it with a Flannery opening. With longer spades, bid them, intending to rebid in hearts if appropriate.
3. No. Flannery shows *exactly* four spades and *exactly* five hearts. I know of players who would open Flannery in third or fourth seat with 4-6 distribution, but I don't recommend it.
4. No. With only 10 HCP and weak suits pass, despite the 2½ quick tricks.
5. Yes. The weak suits do not disqualify this hand from being a Flannery 2 ◊ opening, which is the most descriptive bid available.
6. Yes. The fact that one major suit is much stronger than the other should not deter a 2 ◊ opening.
7. Yes. See Number 6.
8. Yes. A moth-eaten collection containing only 1½ quick tricks, but the strong major suits justify an opening.
9. Yes. 16 HCP is the upper limit for a Flannery opening. This hand does not justify a 1 ♡ opening, followed by a **reverse**. You should pass if partner bids only two of a major after your 2 ◊ opening.
10. No. With strong holdings in three suits 16 HCP and 3½ quick tricks, this hand is worth a reverse. Open 1 ♡. Generally, reverses require 17 or more HCP, and this hand is the exception, not the rule.
11. No. The major suits are strong, but only 12 HCP (including a singleton queen) and 1 quick trick, please pass. Deduct one point when holding a singleton king, queen or jack.

12. Yes. You are certainly not too strong. If partner signs off at 2♡ or 2♠, your very strong suits and 15 HCP justify a game try. (As you will see in Chapter II, you would bid 3◊).

Chapter II

Responding to
Flannery 2 ◊

Chapter II

Responding to Flannery 2 ◊

The Responses

Responding to Flannery seldom presents any serious difficulty. Opener's exact major suit shape is known, and his high card range is limited. Often, responder is able to place the final contract immediately.

The response structure allows sign-offs in every suit: (2♡, 2♠, 3♣ and a pass of 2◊); invitational bids in the majors (3♡ and 3♠); sign-offs in game (4♡, 4♠ and 3 NT); transfers to game (4♣ transfers to 4♡ and 4◊ transfers to 4♠); and two exploratory bids (2 NT and 3◊). The workhorse response is 2 NT, after which opener begins to further describe his hand by showing his exact distribution. All these responses will be described in detail in Chapters II, III and IV.

Responder should add distributional points to his HCP in evaluating his hand. Standard point evaluation is used. With four card support for one of the majors, count:

Doubleton = 1 point
Singleton = 3 points
Void = 5 points

With three card trump support, distributional points are demoted somewhat. Count them as follows:

Doubleton = 1 point
Singleton = 2 points
Void = 3 points

All these point allowances are subject to change as necessary. For example, if you discover that partner has a doubleton opposite your doubleton, no distributional points should be added. Similarly, secondary minor suit honors (queens and jacks) are of dubious value, since partner is likely to be short in the suit.

As a supporting hand, you may also "promote" the value of your fitting cards in hearts and spades if you intend the hand to play in a major suit. Add one extra point to your heart and spade honors if the holdings would otherwise count as less than four points. For example, count:

$$
\begin{aligned}
&K\,x\,x\,(x) &= 4\ (3 + 1\ \text{"promotion"}) \\
&K\,J\,x\,(x) &= 4\ (\text{do not promote beyond 4 points}) \\
&Q\,x\,x\,(x) &= 3\ (2 + 1,\ \text{promotion}) \\
&Q\,J\,x\,(x) &= 4\ (3 + 1,\ \text{promotion}) \\
&J\,x\,x\,(x) &= 2\ (1 + 1,\ \text{promotion}) \\
&A\,Q\,x &= 6\ (\text{do not promote beyond 4}) \\
&10\,x\,x\,x &= 0
\end{aligned}
$$

With fitting honors in both majors, it is possible to promote each suit one point, for a total of two.

Example 1.

♠ Q x x x   ♡ x   ◇ A x x x   ♣ K x x x

Responder has 13 supporting points: 9 HCP; one promotion point for the trump queen; plus three points for the singleton (when holding four trumps). Bid 4♠ in response to 2◇, and expect to make it most of the time, even if partner has a singleton club opposite your king.

Example 2.

♠ x   ♡ K x x   ◇ K Q x x x   ♣ Q x x x

Responder again has 13 supporting points: 10 HCP; one promotion point for the trump king; plus two for the singleton (when holding only three trumps). However, this hand has dangerous waste whenever partner has a singleton diamond. Responder should explore cautiously with an artificial 2 NT bid, and possibly stop in 3 ♡ (see Chapter III for complete coverage of the 2 NT response).

Many more examples in connection with specific responses will be shown later.

The 2♡ and 2♠ Responses

2♡ and 2♠ responses to 2◇ are sign-offs. They may be based on good trump support and minimal values. More often, they are bid as the least of all evils. For example, responder may bid 2♠ with three small spades, or 2♡ with only a doubleton. If the hands fit poorly, responder may have as many as 11 HCP.
Examples of 2♡ and 2♠ responses:

	Opener	*Responder*
Example 1.		

Opener	Responder
♠ A Q x x	♠ K x x
♡ K J 10 x x	♡ x x x
◇ Q x	◇ A x x x
♣ x x	♣ x x x
2 ◇	2 ♡
Pass	

Example 2.

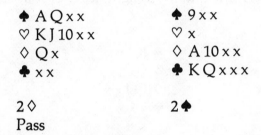

♠ A Q x x   ♠ x
♥ K J 10 x x   ♥ x x
♦ Q x   ♦ J 10 x x x
♣ x x   ♣ A K J x x

2♦   2♥
Pass

Example 3.

♠ A Q x x   ♠ 9 x x
♥ K J 10 x x   ♥ x
♦ Q x   ♦ A 10 x x
♣ x x   ♣ K Q x x x

2♦   2♠
Pass

Opener's Rebid after 2♥ or 2♠

Since responder may have a poor fit and little strength, opener should rarely bid again. His hand is already limited, and responder has available other options if he wishes to explore further. However, if opener's hand is maximum and his suits are strong, he may bid again as a game try. He does so by making the most descriptive bid possible — he bids his longer minor. For example:

	Opener	*Responder*

Example 4.

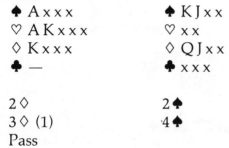

	Opener	*Responder*
♠	A Q x x	♠ x x
♡	K Q J x x	♡ 9 x x x
◊	x	◊ x x x x
♣	K x x	♣ A J 10
	2 ◊	2 ♡
	3 ♣ (1)	4 ♡
	Pass	

(1) Maximum strength; three or four clubs.

Example 5.

	Opener	*Responder*
♠	A x x x	♠ K J x x
♡	A K x x x	♡ x x
◊	K x x x	◊ Q J x x
♣	—	♣ x x x
	2 ◊	2 ♠
	3 ◊ (1)	4 ♠
	Pass	

(1) Maximum strength; three or four diamonds.

In Examples 4 and 5, sound game contracts are reached with minimal values, since responder knows there are no wasted values. If responder's hand were reversed in the above examples, so that the minor suit honors faced shortness in opener's hands, responder would sign off.

Example 6.

Opener	Responder
♠ A Q J x	♠ x x
♡ K Q 10 9 x	♡ x x
◊ x	◊ K x x x
♣ K x x	♣ A Q x x x
2 ◊	2 ♡
3 ♣	Pass

In Example 6, opener's 3♣ game try uncovers the superior club fit. With no interest in game, responder elects to play in 3♣, where there is an eight card fit. This is why you respond in your longer minor. If opener bids his singleton, the club fit is lost on the three-level.

Example 7.

Opener	Responder
♠ A Q J 10	♠ x x x
♡ K Q J x x	♡ x
◊ x	◊ K Q x x x
♣ K x x	♣ J x x x
2 ◊	2 ♠
3 ♣	3 ♠
Pass	

Example 7 demonstrates why opener should ordinarily pass responder's sign-off bid of 2♡ or 2♠. If responder's hand is very weak, or fits poorly, the three-level may be too high.

Example 8.

Opener	Responder
♠ A Q x x	♠ x x
♡ K Q x x x	♡ x x
◇ J	◇ K x x x
♣ K x x	♣ J x x x x
2 ◇	2 ♡
Pass	

In Example 8, opener has 15 HCP but weak suits. Opener's heart suit is not self-sufficient, and responder may have a poor trump fit, as in the example. Since any further bid is fraught with danger, opener wisely passes 2♡. Only maximum hands with strong suits justify further action by opener after a 2♡ or 2♠ response.

Responding with Three Spades and Two Hearts

Holding three spades and two hearts, responder has a choice of whether to play in a 4-3 spade fit or a 5-2 heart fit. There is no hard and fast rule about which is better. Either choice could win on a particular hand. The following considerations are relevant:

1. **Which suit is stronger?** Favor the suit with an honor card. Holding no honors in the majors (that is, three small spades and two small hearts) bid 2♡ to avoid disaster if the hands are something like this:

Opener	Responder
♠ Q x x x	♠ x x x
♡ K Q x x x	♡ x x
◇ A K x	◇ J x x
♣ x	♣ J x x x x

30

Of course, opener could have five small hearts, but he is more likely to have honors in the longer heart suit. Also, the fifth heart is likely to produce an extra trick regardless of bad breaks.

2. **Ruffing values.** If responder's hand contains a singleton or doubleton in a minor, the hand will usually play better in spades. The responding hand can ruff opener's losers. Of course, with 3-2-7-1 or 3-2-1-7 distribution, the longer minor is ofter preferable.

A. ♠ A J x
   ♡ x x
   ◇ x
   ♣ 10 x x x x x x

B. ♠ x x x
   ♡ x x
   ◇ K Q J x x x
   ♣ x x

C. ♠ x x x
   ♡ K 10
   ◇ Q x x x x x x
   ♣ x

D. ♠ x x x
   ♡ K 10
   ◇ x
   ♣ x x x x x x x

Bid 2♠ with hand A. Pass 2◇ with hand B. With hand C, pass 2◇, but with hand D a 2♡ response is preferable to a 3♣ bid.

3. **Honor Cards in the Minors.** Holding honor strength in both minors makes a 2♠ response marginally more attractive than a 2♡ response since there is less danger of being tapped out of trumps. For example:

Opener	*Responder*
♠ A J 9 x	♠ x x x
♡ K Q 9 x x	♡ x x
◇ x	◇ K Q 10 x
♣ K x x	♣ Q J 9 x

The minor suit honors provide delayed stoppers. Respond 2♠ with the hand above based on the minor suit holdings.

The 3♣ Response

The 3♣ response to a Flannery 2◊ opening bid is a sign-off. It is bid with six or more clubs. Generally, the bid is made as the least of all evils since it means that there is no satisfactory fit in the majors and since responder has committed the contract to the three-level. Examples of 3♣ responses to 2◊ openings are:

♠ x x	♠ x x	♠ J x x
♡ x	♡ x	♡ x x
◊ A x x x	◊ A Q x x	◊ x x
♣ K J 10 x x x	♣ Q 9 x x x x	♣ K Q J 10 9 x

If clubs are weak and the hand is potentially a disaster, responder may consider bidding 2♡ with a singleton honor, for example:

Opener	*Responder*
♠ A K x x	♠ x x
♡ K J 9 x x	♡ Q
◊ K x x	◊ A x x x
♣ x	♣ Q x x x x x

2♡ and 2♠ are much more difficult for the opponents to double for penalties, since the auction "sounds" more like a fit, whereas a 3♣ bid is an admission that the hands do not fit well. And, of course, three-level bids are easier for the opponents to double.

Players familiar with Flannery may recall that the 3♣ bid was originally assigned an artificial meaning. Experience has shown that 3♣ is more useful as a sign-off, and that adequate exploration can be made on strong hands with 2 NT and a new special 3◊ response.

Pass of 2 ◇

To sign off in diamonds, you simply pass partner's Flannery opening. The considerations are similar to those for the 3♣ response, and the examples given in the previous section, with the minor suits reversed, are appropriate hands for passing. Since you are one level lower, the pass can occasionally be made with only five diamonds, if you hold specifically 2-1-5-5 distribution. For example:

♠ x x
♡ x
◇ K Q 10 x x
♣ K x x x x

If the major suits were reversed, you would bid 2 ♡ .

You cannot, of course, raise diamonds to show diamonds. The 3 ◇ call is conventional, as you will see in Chapter IV, and has nothing whatsoever to do with the diamond suit. With game interest in diamonds or notrump, bid 2 NT (forcing) to learn more about opener's hand. (See Chapter III). With diamonds, but no interest in game, simply pass 2 ◇ .

The 3 ♡ and 3 ♠ Responses

The 3 ♡ and 3 ♠ responses are invitational to game in the bid suit. They promise a good trump fit (four cards), and imply a good 10 to a poor 12 supporting points. These bids request opener to bid game if his hand is sound (14 or more points) or to pass if it is weak (less than 14 points). Responder is interested in all of opener's high cards, including minor suits. Opener should therefore view minor suit singletons as possible liabilities, since

responder's high cards in the suit will be wasted.
Examples:

Opener	Responder
♠ A 10 x x	♠ K x x x
♡ K Q J x x	♡ x x
◊ K x x	◊ Q J x x
♣ x	♣ K Q x
2 ◊	3 ♠
Pass (1)	
	(1) Only 13 HCP.

♠ K 10 x x	♠ Q x x x
♡ K Q x x x	♡ 10 x
◊ A x	◊ Q J x x
♣ K x	♣ A Q x
2 ◊	3 ♠
4 ♠ (1)	Pass
	(1) 15 HCP.

As an alternative to the 3 ♠ bid on the above hands,
responder could, not unreasonably, bid 2 NT, and "sign-
off in 3 ♠ (as can be seen in Chapter II, opener may
bid game on this sequence with a maximum hand). In
the example hands, the 3 ♠ response is preferable in that it
shows honors in both minors and four trumps. (See
discussion in Chapter III.)

The 4 ♡ and 4 ♠ Responses

4 ♡ and 4 ♠ bids are sign-offs. Opener must pass.
These bids are similar to 4 ♡ or 4 ♠ bids made in response
to a 1 ♡ or 1 ♠ opening. Responder usually hopes to make

the contract, but he might be bidding on a weak, freakish hand. He sees no hope for slam, and elects not to reveal the hands by more scientific exploration. Some examples:

	Opener	Responder
1.	♠ K 10 x x	♠ A 9 x x x
	♡ K Q x x x	♡ x x
	◇ A x x	◇ Q x x
	♣ x	♣ K Q x
	2 ◇	4 ♠
	Pass	
2.	♠ K 10 x x	♠ Q x x
	♡ K Q x x x	♡ A J x x x
	◇ A x x	◇ x
	♣ x	♣ K x x x
	2 ◇	4 ♡
	Pass	
3.	♠ K 10 x x	♠ x
	♡ K Q x x x	♡ 10 x x x
	◇ A x x	◇ Q x x x x x
	♣ x	♣ x x
	2 ◇	4 ♡
	Pass	
4.	♠ K 10 x x	♠ Q x x x x x
	♡ K Q x x x	♡ x
	◇ A x x	◇ K x x x
	♣ x	♣ x x
	2 ◇	4 ♠
	Pass	

As is apparent from the next section, responder could also *transfer* with these hands (4♣ transfers to 4♡ and 4◇ transfers to 4♠). He does not transfer in Examples 1, 2 and 4 because these hands have possible lead value.

In Example 3, the diamond queen may have lead value, but the primary reason for not transferring is to prevent the opponents from doubling 4♣ and finding their big club fit.

Further analysis of when to transfer, and when not to, is found in the next section.

The 4♣ and 4 Diamond Responses

A 4♣ response to a 2◇ opening bid is a transfer to 4♡. A 4◇ response to 2◇ is a transfer to 4♠. Like direct responses of 4♡ and 4♠, these bids are ambiguous. Usually, there will be a fair probability that the contract will make, but responder may have a weak, freakish hand.

Responder has complete discretion whether to transfer or to play game himself. He should generally transfer if his hand contains no tenaces (for example, Kx, AQx, KJx), since his partner's hand might contain such holdings.

Over the years, I have found that transfer responses gain, not only because they protect opener's tenaces, but because they conceal opener's minor suit distribution. This makes it more difficult for the opponents to cash out their winners in the correct order. For example:

1.
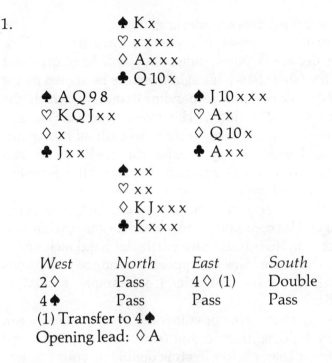

West	North	East	South
2 ◇	Pass	4 ◇ (1)	Double
4 ♠	Pass	Pass	Pass

(1) Transfer to 4 ♠
Opening lead: ◇ A

If North continues diamonds, West will make his contract with an overtrick by driving out trumps and then discarding East's clubs on the long hearts. A club shift wins for the defense on this layout, but not if West holds either of the hands below:

2. ♠ A Q x x   3. ♠ A x x x
    ♡ Q 10 9 x x   ♡ K Q J x x
    ◇ x x   ◇ x x x
    ♣ K J   ♣ K

Expert defenders playing count signals — rather than the standard attitude signals which the majority of players would use in this situation — would probably succeed in Example 2 when they determine that declarer has an even number of diamonds (probably two). But the ambiguity between one and three diamonds in Examples 1 and 3 would leave the defenders guessing.

Of course, as soon as defenders do learn the length of either of declarer's minor suits, they will have an exact count of the whole hand. It might therefore be argued that it is better to conceal the responding hand, of which the defenders know nothing. However, against Flannery hands, the winning defense often is to cash all minor suit winners and wait for your major suit tricks which can seldom be discarded completely. Exposing the Flannery hand as dummy facilitates the cash-out defense.

Please do not use a transfer simply because it is an available gadget. Use common sense instead. Some reasons you might not want to transfer on a particular hand include:

1.   Your hand contains unsupported honor combinations which may have lead value (for example, Kx, AQx, or KJx).

2.   The opponents are not vulnerable, you are very weak in the artificial transfer suit (clubs or diamonds), and you fear that a lead-directing double of your transfer bid may enable the opponents to find a cheap sacrifice, or even a makable game.

The 3 NT Response

3 NT is to play, expecting to make. The responding hand may be unbalanced, since it is frequently short in the major suits.

Be careful about bidding 3 NT on thin values when your minor suits are weak.

Examples of 3 NT responses:

1. | Opener | Responder |
    |---|---|
    | ♠ K 10 x x | ♠ Q x |
    | ♡ K Q x x x | ♡ A |
    | ◊ A x x | ◊ K Q x x x |
    | ♣ x | ♣ K 10 9 x x |
    | | |
    | 2 ◊ | 3 NT |
    | Pass | |

2. | Opener | Responder |
    |---|---|
    | ♠ K 10 x x | ♠ Q x |
    | ♡ K Q x x x | ♡ x |
    | ◊ A x x | ◊ K Q J 10 9 x |
    | ♣ x | ♣ A Q x x |
    | | |
    | 2 ◊ | 3 NT |
    | Pass | |

3. | Opener | Responder |
    |---|---|
    | ♠ K 10 x x | ♠ A Q x |
    | ♡ K Q x x x | ♡ J x |
    | ◊ A x x | ◊ K Q 10 x |
    | ♣ x | ♣ Q J 9 8 |
    | | |
    | 2 ◊ | 3 NT |
    | Pass | |

QUIZ

Chapter II
Responses

As responder, what do you bid with the following hands after partner opens Flannery 2 ◊ ?

1. ♠ x
   ♡ J x
   ◊ K x x x x
   ♣ A x x x x

2. ♠ Q x
   ♡ x
   ◊ K Q x x x
   ♣ x x x x x

3. ♠ 9 x x
   ♡ A x
   ◊ Q x x
   ♣ K x x x

4. ♠ 9 x x x
   ♡ 10 x x
   ◊ Q x x x
   ♣ A x

5. ♠ A x x x
   ♡ Q x
   ◊ A x x x
   ♣ x x x

6. ♠ Q x x x x
   ♡ x
   ◊ A x x x
   ♣ K x x

7. ♠ x x
   ♡ x
   ◊ J x x x
   ♣ K 10 9 x x x

8. ♠ x x
   ♡ x
   ◊ K 10 9 x x x
   ♣ J x x x

9. ♠ x
   ♡ x x
   ◊ K 10 x x x x
   ♣ J x x x

10. ♠ x
    ♡ x x
    ◊ K x x x
    ♣ K Q J 10 x x

11. ♠ Q x x x x x
    ♡ x
    ◊ K Q x
    ♣ x x x

12. ♠ A x x x
    ♡ A J x
    ◊ x x x
    ♣ x x x

13. ♠ Q x x
    ♡ x
    ◊ K J 10 x x x
    ♣ K x x

14. ♠ Q x x x
    ♡ x
    ◊ K J 10 x x x
    ♣ K x

15. ♠ 10 x x x
    ♡ x x x
    ◊ A Q x
    ♣ K Q x

16. ♠ Q
    ♡ x x
    ◇ A Q J 10 x x
    ♣ K Q 9 x

17. ♠ J x
    ♡ Q
    ◇ K Q J x x
    ♣ A 10 9 x x

18. ♠ K x x
    ♡ x x
    ◇ K J x x
    ♣ J 10 9 8

ANSWERS TO CHAPTER II QUIZ

1. 2 ♡   Sign-off.
2. Pass   The least of all evils.
3. 2 ♡   Bid the major with the honor.
4. 2 ♠   The 4-4 fit (spades) is generally better than a 5-3 heart fit, since the five card suit may provide a place to pitch side suit losers.
5. 2 NT   Lacking honors in both minors.
6. 4 ♠   Don't transfer, you want the lead up to your hand.
7. 3 ♣   The best bid possible.
8. Pass   To play.
9. Pass   This hand might be useless in hearts.
10. 3 ♣   Sign-off.
11. 4 ♢   Transfer to 4 ♠.
12. 2 NT   Based on good major suit holdings.
13. Pass   A close decision. Bid 2 ♠ without the diamond jack.
14. 4 ♠   You want the lead coming up to your hand.
15. 3 ♠   Shows honors in both minors and four spades.
16. 3 NT   With weak majors and strong minors, bid 3 NT.
17. 3 NT   With weak majors and strong minors, bid 3 NT.
18. 2 ♠   Compare with Question 3.

Chapter III

The 2 NT Response

Chapter III

The 2 NT Response

2 NT is the most important and most frequently used response to the Flannery 2 ◊ opening. It is artificial and forcing. The 2 NT bidder says nothing about his hand, except that he has interest in game or slam. He can, therefore, have as little as a good 10 supporting points or an unlimited maximum; balanced or unbalanced distribution; and he may or may not have a good fit with opener's major suits.

2 NT asks opener to describe his hand further. Opener never counts distributional points when responding to 2 NT; he counts HCP only. Responder will learn opener's exact distribution and will be in a good position to judge whether opener's HCP are all working. Responder counts his own distributional points as a supporting hand.

The 2 NT response is forcing, and has the same meaning even when responder has previously passed.

The responses to 2 NT are as follows:

Opener's Rebid after 2 NT

Opener's first rebid after 2 NT defines his exact shape. If opener has doubletons in both minors (4-5-2-2 distribution), his first rebid also narrows his HCP range.

Specifically, opener rebids as follows:

3 ♣ = exactly three clubs (4-5-1-3 distribution).
3 ◊ = exactly three diamonds (4-5-3-1 distribution).

44

3♡ = doubletons in both minors and MINIMUM HCP (11 to a poor 14 HCP).

3♠ = doubletons in both minors; MAXIMUM HCP (good 14 to 16 HCP); strength is concentrated in the major suits.

3NT = doubletons in both minors; MAXIMUM HCP; honors in both minors, Qx or better.

4♣ = four clubs (4-5-0-4 distribution).

4♢ = four diamonds (4-5-4-0 distribution).

All these bids are described in detail below. For convenience, the responses showing doubletons will be discussed first.

Responses to 2 NT

The 3♡ Rebid by Opener

The 3♡ rebid after 2 NT shows 4-5-2-2 distribution and minimum point count. Hands with 11 to 13 HCP are considered minimum. Hands with 14 HCP may be minimum or maximum. Fourteen point hands with strong major suits (honors heading the suits and good spot cards) or hands rich in quick tricks are upgraded. Hands with poor suits, considerable honor strength in the doubletons, or "soft" values (queens and jacks) are downgraded.

Typical hands on which opener would rebid 3♡:

1. ♠ Kxxx
   ♡ AQxxx
   ♢ Kx
   ♣ xx

2. ♠ QJxx
   ♡ KJxxx
   ♢ KQ
   ♣ Qx

3. ♠ AKQx
   ♡ xxxxx
   ♢ Ax
   ♣ xx

Hand 1 has 2½ quick tricks, but only 12 HCP.
Hand 2 has 14 HCP, but must be downgraded, because

45

of indifferent suit quality and minimum quick tricks.

Hand 3 is a "maximum" minimum. If the AKQ headed the five card heart suit instead of spades, the hand would be upgraded to a 3♠ response, even though it has only 13 HCP.

Responder's Rebid after Opener's 3♡ Minimum Bid

Sign-Offs

If responder has a poor 12 supporting points or less, he signs off after a 3♡ response. He may do so by passing opener in 3♡ or by bidding 3♠, which opener must pass (responder is simply choosing the major suit in which he has a fit). The hands might be one of the following:

	Opener	Responder
1.	♠ K x x x	♠ A x x
	♡ A Q x x x	♡ J x x
	◇ K x	◇ A x x x
	♣ x x	♣ Q x x
	2 ◇	2 NT
	3 ♡	Pass
2.	♠ K x x x	♠ A x x x
	♡ A Q x x x	♡ J x
	◇ K x	◇ x x x
	♣ x x	♣ A Q x x
	2 ◇	2 NT
	3 ♡	3 ♠
	Pass	

All game bids by responder are also sign-offs.

Opener	Responder
2 ◊	2 NT
3 ♡	3 NT, 4 ♡, 4 ♠, 5 ♣ or 5 ◊

are all sign-offs.

Slam Tries

Responder may explore for slam by bidding 4 NT (Blackwood), or by cue bidding 4 ♣ or 4 ◊. These cue bids imply first round control (ace or void). OPENER MUST NOT PASS. In fact, this rule applies to *all* sequences beginning 2 ◊ - 2 NT.

RULE: After a 2 NT response to Flannery, opener can never pass responder in four of a minor.

Continuations after Responder Cue Bids

Although cue bidding is not the subject of this book, for completeness here are two examples of cue bidding sequences following opener's 3 ♡ rebid:

	Opener	Responder
1.	♠ K J x x	♠ A Q 9 x x
	♡ K x x x x	♡ A Q
	◊ A x	◊ x x x x x
	♣ x x	♣ A
	2 ◊	2 NT
	3 ♡	4 ♣ (1)
	4 ◊ (1)	6 ♠
	Pass	

(1) Cue bid

2.   ♠ K J x x   ♠ A Q 9 x x
      ♡ K x x x x   ♡ A Q
      ◊ x x   ◊ A
      ♣ A x   ♣ x x x x x

      2 ◊   2 NT
      3 ♡   4 ◊ (1)
      4 ♡   5 ◊ (1)
      6 ♣ (1)   6 ♠
      Pass

      (1) Cue bid

In Example 1, opener's 4 ◊ cue bid does not suggest extra values, since opener has not by-passed four of a major. His cue bid is mandatory. In Example 2, opener elects not to bid beyond the four-level, since he has only 11 HCP, two quick tricks, and broken suits. When responder persists with 5 ◊ (showing second round control), opener finally shows his club ace. With a better hand (which cannot exceed a poor 14 HCP after his 3 ♡ rebid), opener would have cue bid 5 ♣ directly over 4 ◊ .

Having started a cue bidding sequence, responder cannot sign off in five of a minor. Opener assumes there is an implied fit in one of the majors. Responder could, of course, have signed off by bidding five of a minor directly over opener's 3 ♡ rebid.

The 3 ♠ Rebid by Opener

The 3 ♠ rebid after 2 NT shows: 4-5-2-2 distribution; maximum point count (a good 14 to 16 HCP); and high card strength concentrated in the long suits (at least one of the minors will be Jx or xx).

Examples of 3 ♠ rebids after 2 NT:

1. ♠ K Q 10 x   2. ♠ K Q 10 x   3. ♠ Q J 10 x
   ♡ A J 10 x x   ♡ A Q J x x   ♡ A K Q x x
   ◇ A J   ◇ K x   ◇ x x
   ♣ x x   ♣ x x   ♣ K x

4. ♠ A K 10 9   5. ♠ K J 10 x   6. ♠ A K J x
   ♡ A K 10 9 x   ♡ A Q J x x   ♡ K Q J x x
   ◇ x x   ◇ A x   ◇ Q x
   ♣ x x   ♣ x x   ♣ x x

7. ♠ x x x x
   ♡ A K J x x
   ◇ A K
   ♣ x x

After the 3 ♠ bid, responder can place the contract by bidding 3 NT, 4 ◇, 4 ♠, 5 ♣ or 5 ◇, or he can cue bid 4 ♣ or 4 ◇ or bid 4 NT as Blackwood. These bids have the same meaning as when opener rebids 3 ◇.

The 3 NT Rebid by Opener

The 3 NT rebid after the 2 NT inquiry shows 4-5-2-2 distribution; maximum values (a good 14 to 16 HCP); *and* concentrated strength in the minors. Typically, opener holds at least 4 HCP in the minors and usually more. There must be a minimum of Qx in each minor. Opener cannot have a worthless doubleton.

Examples of 3 NT rebids by opener in response to 2 NT:

1. ♠ A 10 x x   2. ♠ J 10 9 x   3. ♠ K Q 9 x
   ♡ K Q x x x   ♡ K x x x x   ♡ Q 10 9 x x
   ◇ A x   ◇ A Q   ◇ Q x
   ♣ K x   ♣ A J   ♣ A Q

4. ♠ Q J 9 x   5. ♠ A Q x x   6. ♠ K J x x
    ♡ K Q 10 8 x   ♡ Q J 10 x x   ♡ A 10 x x x
    ◇ K x   ◇ Q x   ◇ K x
    ♣ A x   ♣ A 10   ♣ A x

7. ♠ Q J 10 x
    ♡ Q J 10 8 x
    ◇ A 10
    ♣ A x

Responder's rebids are the same as those following the 3♡ and 3♠ responses. He can pass; bid 4♡, 4♠, 5♣ or 5◇ to play; cue bid 4♣ or 4◇; or bid 4 NT, Blackwood. The auction might proceed as follows:

Opener	Responder
♠ A 10 x x	♠ J 9 x
♡ K Q x x x	♡ J
◇ A x	◇ K Q J x x
♣ K x	♣ Q J 10 x
2 ◇	2 NT
3 NT	Pass

Or, as in the following hand:

♠ J 10 9 8	♠ A K x
♡ K x x x x	♡ A x x x x
◇ A Q	◇ K x x
♣ A J	♣ x x
2 ◇	2 NT
3 NT	4 ◇ (1)
5 ♣ (1)	6 ♡
Pass	

(1) Cue bid

Responder's 4 ◇ cue bid would ordinarily show the ace, but he had no ace to bid (4 ♡ and 4 ♠ are sign-offs).

The 3 ♣ and 3 ◇ Rebids by Opener

The 3 ♣ rebid after 2 NT shows three clubs (4-5-1-3 distribution). The 3 ◇ rebid after 2 NT shows three diamonds (4-5-3-1 distribution). It is easy to remember since the bid says, literally, how many cards you have in the bid suit.

Note that the 3 ♣ and 3 ◇ responses give no indication of opener's strength. Generally, knowledge of opener's exact shape is the most important information, since responder can determine how well the hands fit. For example, a holding of KQx opposite partner's singleton is a red flag that the hands do not fit well. Responder should therefore downgrade his expectations for the hand such as by stopping at the three-level or giving up on slam aspirations, as the case may be. Alternatively, if responder holds Axx or three small cards in opener's short suit, he knows that the hands fit well indeed in that there are no wasted values. Accordingly, he can press on to game or slam on what would otherwise be doubtful values. As will be seen, responder can, if necessary, inquire further to learn opener's point range as well.

First, here are examples of the 3 ♣ and 3 ◇ responses in action:

	Opener	Responder
1.	♠ A x x x	♠ K x x x
	♡ K Q J x x	♡ A x
	◇ K x x	◇ Q J x x
	♣ x	♣ x x x
	2 ◇	2 NT
	3 ◇	4 ♠
	Pass	

With fitting cards in both majors, responder tries for game with only 10 HCP. Discovering partner's singleton club, he confidently bids an excellent game on a combined holding of 23 HCP.

2.	♠ A x x x	♠ K x x x
	♡ K Q J x x	♡ A x
	◇ x	◇ Q J x x
	♣ K x x	♣ x x x
	2 ◇	2 NT
	3 ♣	3 ♠
	Pass	

Example 2 is identical to Example 1, except that opener's minor suit holdings are reversed. Responder knows, in Example 2, that his diamond queen and jack are virtually worthless opposite opener's singleton, so he signs off in 3 ♠. With a maximum opener can bid 4 ♠. With only 13 HCP he passes. This brings us to opener's second rebid after first rebidding 3 ♣ or 3 ◇.

Opener's Rebid after Responding 3 ♣ or 3 ◇ to a 2 NT Inquiry from Responder

Most of the time, responder (the 2 NT bidder) will take charge of the auction, and opener will have little or no discretion. If necessary, responder may ascertain opener's point count by bidding 4 ♣ (to be explained later in this chapter), check for aces by bidding 4 NT, Blackwood, or both. However, when responder bids 3 ♡ or 3 ♠, the final decision rests with the opener, because responder does not know opener's precise point range.

(a) When Responder "Signs-Off" in 3 ♡ or 3 ♠

Frequently, responder will "sign-off" in 3 ♡ or 3 ♠ after hearing opener's 3 ♣ or 3 ◇ rebid to 2 NT. These bids imply a good 10 to a poor 12 supporting points, and suggest that there are, or are likely to be, wasted values. Typically, responder has honor strength opposite opener's singleton. Sometimes, there will be relatively little wasted values, but responder's 10 to 12 points hand is simply too weak to insist on game unless opener has a maximum, or near maximum, hand. The 3 ♡ and 3 ♠ rebids are, therefore, not true sign-offs. Opener is not compelled to pass, and in fact, is expected to bid on to game in the agreed suit with 15-16 HCP or with a 14 point hand containing good suit quality.

Compare these two auctions:

	Opener	Responder
(1)	2 ◇	2 NT
	3 ♣	3 ♠
	?	
(2)	2 ◇	2 NT
	3 ♡	3 ♠
	Pass	

In the first example, opener bids again with the good 14 to 16 HCP hands, and passes, otherwise. In the second example, where opener has rebid 3 ♡, showing a minimum hand, he must pass. The reason for this is obvious. The 3 ♡ response not only defined opener's shape, but also limited his strength (opener would have bid 3 ♠ or 3 NT with a better hand). In contrast, the 3 ♣ (or 3 ◇) bid only defined opener's shape — it did not narrow his HCP range, which might vary between 11 and 16 HCP. Responder is forced to assume opener's hand is near the bottom of that range, so that the partnership does not get overboard on insufficient values. It is opener's duty to carry on to game if he has better than average values.

Following are some examples of minimum (11 to a poor 14 HCP) hands with which opener should pass responder's 3♡ or 3♠ rebid:

1. ♠ A Q x x
   ♡ K Q x x x
   ◇ Q x x
   ♣ x

2. ♠ A Q J x
   ♡ K Q 10 9 x
   ◇ x x x
   ♣ x

3. ♠ x x x x
   ♡ A K Q x x
   ◇ x
   ♣ K x x

4. ♠ K 10 9 x
   ♡ Q 10 9 x x
   ◇ A Q x
   ♣ Q

Following are some examples of maximum (a good 14 to 16 HCP) hands with which opener should raise responder's 3♡ or 3♠ rebid:

1. ♠ A K x x
   ♡ A K J x x
   ◇ x x x
   ♣ x

2. ♠ K 10 x x
   ♡ A Q J x x
   ◇ A 10 x
   ♣ x

3. ♠ K x x x
   ♡ A x x x x
   ◇ K J x
   ♣ A

4. ♠ A K 10 x
   ♡ Q J 10 x x
   ◇ x
   ♣ K J 9

When the decision of whether to carry on to game is close, the quality of the holding in the trump suit, as opposed to the other major, might be decisive. For example, on the following hand, opener would raise responder's 3♡ bid to four, based on the strong holding in the agreed suit, but would pass a 3♠ bid by responder.

♠ x x x x
♡ A K J 10 7
◊ A Q 9
♣ x

If partner's hand is

♠ A x
♡ 9 x x x
◊ J 10 x
♣ K Q x x

4♡ is a favorite to make. On the other hand, if partner holds

♠ A x x x
♡ 9 x
◊ J 10 x
♣ K Q x x

4♠ is doubtful.

Similarly, on the following hand, opener should pass a 3♡ bid by responder but raise a 3♠ bid to four.

♠ K Q J x
♡ Q x x x x
◊ A Q x
♣ x

Opener bids 4♠, hoping responder's hand is something like the hands below:

1. ♠ A x x x
    ♡ K x
    ◊ J x x x
    ♣ K x x

2. ♠ A x x x
    ♡ A x
    ◊ J x x x
    ♣ Q x x

If, on the other hand, responder had bid 3♡ with either of the hands below game would not be fun.

3. ♠ A x
    ♡ K x x
    ◊ J 10 x x
    ♣ K x x x

4. ♠ x x
    ♡ A x x
    ◊ K J x x
    ♣ K x x x

Finally, note that responder has two methods of inviting game in a major suit. He may bid 3♡ or 3♠ directly over 2◊, without bidding 2 NT, or he may bid 2 NT, and, if opener rebids 3♣ or 3◊, follow up with a 3♡ or 3♠ rebid. Both auctions show the same values. However, the immediate response of 3♡ or 3♠ is rare. 2 NT is usually preferable in that it allows responder to evaluate his minor suit holdings in light of opener's proven distribution. Thus, the 2 NT sequence tends to minimize guesswork.

Nevertheless, the immediate 3♡ or 3♠ responses do have their uses. They show four card trump support (the 2 NT sequence could be based on three card support) and suggest fair values in both minors. Opener is expected to give full weight to all minor suit honors in evaluating his hand. Even singleton honors will not be entirely worthless. In comparison, the 2 NT response is especially useful when responder has a concentration of strength in one minor, and a holding such as Axx, or all small cards, in the other. On those types of hands, the location of opener's singleton, if any, is of paramount importance.

You may find it useful at this point to review the discussion of the immediate 3♡ and 3♠ responses in Chapter II.

(b) When Responder Signs Off in 3 NT, 4♡, 4♠, 5♣, 5♢ and all Slams

After learning opener's exact shape from the 2 NT inquiry, responder will often be able to place the final contract immediately by bidding game, or even slam. Opener *must* pass these bids, even with a tip-top maximum. Responder could have explored further if he wanted to, as will be demonstrated below. By bidding game or slam, he denies all interest in opener's maximum values.

(c) When Responder Bids 4♣ (Strength Asking)

After bidding 2 NT and receiving a 3♣ or 3♢ response, responder will know whether the hands fit well, but still may not know whether the partnership holds sufficient strength for slam. Remember, the 3♣ and 3♢ responses show as few as 11, and as many as 16, HCP. To find out opener's strength, responder simply bids 4♣. Opener rebids as follows:

    4♢ = MINIMUM (11 to a poor 14 HCP)
    4♡ = MAXIMUM (a good 14 to 16 HCP)

With a poor hand and/or few quick tricks, opener must warn partner by bidding 4♢, even if his hand has 14 HCP. Opener devalues any singleton honor, except the singleton ace. Subtract one point for a singleton king, queen or jack. This is not an exact science, but responder will be much more interested in honors in your other three suits.

As always, opener does *not* count distributional points.

Please note that the strength asking bid of 4♣ applies in only two sequences:

	Opener	Responder
1.	2♦	2 NT
	3♣	4♣

and

2.	2♦	2 NT
	3♦	4♣

Note that 4♣ is not needed as a strength asking bid after a 3♡, 3♠ or 3 NT response to 2 NT, as those bids already show opener's strength, along with his distribution. After responses of 3♡, 3♠ or 3 NT to responder's 2 NT, 4♣ is, therefore, a cue bid, not strength asking. Also, do not confuse this sequence with a direct 4♣ bid not preceded by 2 NT (2♦ - 4♣), which is a transfer (See Chapter II). Finally, this strength asking bid does not apply if the 3♣ or 3♦ response is doubled. 4♣ and 4♦ are then needed as transfer bids, so that opener's minor suit is not led through. This is explained in Chapter IV.

Although use of the 4♣ bid as a strength asking bid is limited to those hands in which opener's shape is 4-5-1-3 or 4-5-3-1, it is a very valuable tool. This often makes slam bidding a cinch. For example:

	Opener	*Responder*
1.	♠ K Q x x	♠ A J
	♡ K Q 10 x x	♡ A J x x
	◊ Q x x	◊ J 10 x x
	♣ x	♣ A x x

Opener	Responder
2 ◊	2 NT
3 ◊	4 ♣ (1)
4 ◊ (2)	4 ♡
Pass	

(1) Strength asking
(2) Minimum — 11 to a poor 14 HCP

	Opener	*Responder*
2.	♠ K Q x x	♠ A J
	♡ K Q x x x	♡ A J x x
	◊ K Q x	◊ J 10 x x
	♣ x	♣ A x x

Opener	Responder
2 ◊	2 NT
3 ◊	4 ♣ (1)
4 ♡ (2)	6 ♡
Pass	

(1) Strength asking
(2) Maximum — a good 14 to 16 HCP

Responder's hand is identical in both examples. Although a minimum, with a good fit in both majors and three aces, he explores the slam possibilites. Opener's 3 ◊ rebid is encouraging to responder, as it means there is likely to be no waste in clubs, so responder bids 4 ♣ to ask for strength. In Hand 1 opener shows a minimum, and responder signs off. But in Hand 2 opener's maximum is all responder needs to bid a laydown slam. From responder's point of view, opener must have at least the king in the diamond suit. With

♠ K Q x x
♡ K Q x x x
◊ Q x x
♣ K

opener would demote the club king and count his hand as only 14 HCP.

The above example might appear too perfect. Obviously, the 4♣ inquiry is not always so effective at proving whether slam is a good bet. However, it almost always helps responder exercise good slam judgment. For example:

Opener	Responder
♠ K x x x	♠ A Q x
♡ A Q 10 x x	♡ K x x x x
◊ A Q x	◊ K x x
♣ x	♣ K J
2 ◊	2 NT
3 ◊	4 ♣ (1)
4 ♡ (2)	4 NT
5 ♡	6 ♡
Pass	

(1) Strength asking
(2) Maximum, a good 14 to 16 HCP

Responder's club values are unlikely to pull their full weight opposite opener's singleton, but with a strong fit for both majors, responder tries for slam. After finding a maximum, responder checks for aces, just to be sure. The final contract is a laydown.

The 4♣ and 4♦ Rebid by Opener

After 2♦ - 2 NT, opener shows a 4-5-4-0 or 4-5-0-4 distribution by bidding his four card minor suit at the four level. The bids mean just what they say: 4♣ shows four clubs and 4♦ shows four diamonds.

The 4♣ and 4♦ responses do not promise any particular strength. Opener may be minimum or maximum. As a practical matter, opener's point range is limited somewhat from 11 to a not-too-robust 15 HCP. With more, the 4-5-4-0 or 4-5-0-4 shape would justify a reverse.

Do not make the mistake of rebidding only 3♣ or 3♦ with 4-5-4-0 or 4-5-0-4 shape because your hand is minimum. Partner promises sufficient values for his 2 NT inquiry that a four level contract is unlikely to be in jeopardy. The only time to consider ever lying by bidding only 3♣ or 3♦ is if partner is a passed hand and you opened light in third or fourth seat.

Probably, the value of partner's hand will depend on which minor suit you have, and your conservative call is unlikely to mislead. Besides, with partner's hand limited by his prior pass, you need not fear that a slam will be missed. Of course, if you have a sound hand for your third or fourth seat opener, make the normal systemic response of 4♣ or 4♦.

There are no special rebids applicable to auctions in which opener shows a 4-5-4-0 or 4-5-0-4 distribution. The only ambiguous situation is where responder bids opener's void. For simplicity, treat the 4♣ and 4♦ responses to 2 NT as forcing to game, except that responder, who is captain of the ship, may pass on hands such as the following:

Opener	Responder
♠ A K x x	♠ x x x
♡ K x x x x	♡ Q
◇ —	◇ A K J x x
♣ J x x	♣ Q 10 x x

2 ◇	2 NT
4 ♣	Pass!

Opener is forced to bid if responder calls 4 ◇ over his 4 ♣ bid:

2 ◇	2 NT
4 ♣	4 ◇ (forcing)

I have given this bid no special definition, and treat it simply as a slam try. If opener has a good hand, he can bid 5 ◇ or 5 ♡. Otherwise, he signs off in 4 ♡, allowing responder to correct to the best contract. A regular partnership may wish to assign a special meaning to this 4 ◇ rebid by responder (such as control-asking or point-count asking).

In contrast to the 4 ◇ bid after 4 ♣, a 5 ♣ call after 4 ◇ must be passed. Partner wants to play there, or at least he cannot think of a better contract. Certainly he can't complain about your trump support. You never promised him any!

The hands may be something like this:

Opener	Responder
♠ Q x x x	♠ x
♡ A K J 10 x	♡ x
◇ K x x x	◇ A x x x
♣ —	♣ K Q J 10 9 x x
2 ◇	2 NT
4 ◇	5 ♣
Pass	

4 NT Blackwood

4 NT is always Blackwood on auctions in which responder first bids 2 NT. It is irrelevant whether responder made other bids prior to bidding 4 NT (such as the 4 ♣ strength asking after a 3 ♣ or 3 ◇ rebid by opener).

QUIZ TO CHAPTER III

State the meaning of the last bid and whether it is forcing.

	Opener	Responder		Opener	Responder
1.	2 ◇	2 NT	11.	2 ◇	2 NT
	3 ♡	3 ♠		3 ◇	4 ♣
				4 ◇	4 ♠
2.	2 ◇	2 NT	12.	2 ◇	2 NT
	3 ♣	3 ♠		4 ◇	4 NT
3.	2 ◇	2 NT	13.	2 ◇	2 NT
	3 NT			3 NT	4 NT
4.	2 ◇	2 NT	14.	2 ◇	4 NT
	3 ♠	4 ♣			
5.	2 ◇	2 NT	15.	Pass	2 ◇
	3 NT	4 ♣		2 NT	
6.	2 ◇	2 NT	16.	2 ◇	2 NT
	3 ◇	4 ♣		3 ♣	4 ♣
7.	2 ◇	2 NT	17.	2 ◇	2 NT
	4 ♣	4 ◇		4 ♡	
8.	2 ◇	2 NT	18.	2 ◇	2 NT
	4 ◇	5 ♣		3 ♣	5 ◇
9.	2 ◇	2 NT	19.	2 ◇	2 NT
	4 ◇			3 ♡	4 ♣
10.	2 ◇	3 ♠	20.	2 ◇	2 NT
				3 ♡	4 ◇

ANSWERS TO CHAPTER III QUIZ

1. Sign-off. Opener must pass.
2. Sign-off, but opener should bid again with a good hand.
3. 4-5-2-2, 15-16 HCP, strength in both minors, not forcing.
4. Cue bid. Opener should bid 4 $\diamond$ with the ace, otherwise, 4 $\heartsuit$.
5. Cue bid.
6. Strength asking.
7. Forcing; slam try.
8. To play.
9. Shows four diamonds and a void in clubs.
10. Invitational; four spades, strength in both minors.
11. Sign-off.
12. Blackwood.
13. Blackwood.
14. Blackwood.
15. Forcing. Same as if responder hadn't passed.
16. Strength asking.
17. Opener has four spades and six hearts. I do not recommend bidding Flannery with this holding.
18. To play.
19. Cue bid.
20. Cue bid.

Chapter IV

Innovations and Defensive Strategy

Chapter IV

Innovations and Defensive Strategy

The Three Diamond Response

The original meaning of a 3 ◊ response to a 2 ◊ opening was to ask opener to bid 3 NT with a diamond honor. The purpose of this bid was to enable the responder to be assured that his long diamond suit was solidified by opener or to enable the partnership to locate a diamond stopper so that 3 NT could be reached. Experience has demonstrated that this bid rarely came up. Consequently a new and more useful structure is now recommended as follows:

A 3 ◊ response to a 2 ◊ opening asks for major suit controls. Controls are defined as the ace, king or queen. Opener's first bid shows the number of controls that he possesses in spades. If responder wants to inquire about opener's heart controls, he bids the next step, i.e., the lowest possible bid, over opener's response to the 3 ◊ inquiry. The scheme works like this:

THE 3 ◇ INQUIRY AND RESPONSES

The Spade Control Inquiry

Opener	Responder
2 ◇	3 ◇ (1)
3 ♡ (2)	
3 ♠ (3)	
3 NT (4)	
4 ♣ (5)	

(1) Asking about the number of spade controls.
(2) One spade control (either the ace, king or queen).
(3) Two spade controls.
(4) Three spade controls.
(5) No spade controls.

The Heart Control Inquiry

Opener	Responder
2 ◇	3 ◇

If Opener Responds	Then
3 ♡	3 ♠ asks for the heart controls.
3 ♠	3 NT asks for the heart controls.
3 NT	4 ♣ asks for the heart controls.
4 ♣	4 ◇ asks for the heart controls.

Opener's responses to the heart control inquiry are analogous to his responses to the spade control inquiry, i.e., a four step process with the first step showing one control, the second step two controls, the third step three controls and the fourth step no controls.

Responder uses the 3 ◇ inquiry only when he has slam interest and a first or second round control (ace, king, singleton or void) in each minor.

Example 1.

Opener	Responder
♠ K J 8 2	♠ A Q 5
♡ A Q 10 6 3	♡ K 9 5 4
◇ 8 4	◇ A K J 7 3
♣ Q 8	♣ 5
2 ◇	3 ◇ (1)
3 ♡ (2)	3 ♠ (3)
4 ♣ (4)	4 NT (5)
5 ◇	6 ♡

(1) Asking for the number of spade controls.
(2) One spade control.
(3) Asking for heart controls.
(4) Two heart controls.
(5) Blackwood.

By bidding 3 ◇, responder was able to discover that opener had the spade king, the heart ace and the heart queen. When responder bid 4 NT, Blackwood, he was prepared to bid 6 ♡ if opener showed one ace or to bid 7 ♡ if opener had shown up with two aces.

Example 2.

Following is a hand from a club game. Using the new 3 ◇ bid, responder was able to bid the slam knowing that it is virtually a laydown.

Opener	Responder
♠ Q 8 7 6	♠ K 5
♡ A K Q 8 3	♡ 10 6 5 2
◇ A 4	◇ 9
♣ 7 6	♣ A K Q 8 4 2

2 ◇	3 ◇ (1)
3 ♡ (2)	3 ♠ (3)
4 ◇ (4)	4 NT (5)
5 ♡	6 ♡

(1) Asking for the number of spade controls.
(2) One spade control.
(3) Asking for heart controls.
(4) Three heart controls.
(5) Blackwood.

Responder knew that Opener had the AKQ of hearts and either the ace of spades or the queen of spades and the ace of diamonds.

Example 3.

Opener	Responder
♠ 9 7 5 2	♠ K 6
♡ A K 7 6 4	♡ Q 9 5 3
◇ A 9 6	◇ K 8
♣ 5	♣ A K Q 8 6

2 ◇	3 ◇ (1)
4 ♣ (2)	4 ◇ (3)
4 ♠ (4)	4 NT (5)
5 ♡	6 ♡

(1) Asking for the number of spade controls.
(2) No spade controls.

(3) Asking for heart controls.
(4) Two heart controls.
(5) Blackwood.

After discovering that Opener had two heart controls but no spade controls, responder checked for aces. When Opener showed two aces, he bid the slam knowing that the slam would depend at worst on the location of the ace of spades. If a spade is not led, the club suit may provide discards for the spade suit.

Example 4.

Opener	Responder
♠ A J 10 6	♠ 8 3 2
♡ A J 9 7 2	♡ K 8 6
◊ Q 6	◊ K 3
♣ J 8	♣ A K Q 9 5
2 ◊	3 ◊ (1)
3 ♡ (2)	3 ♠ (3)
3 NT (4)	4 ♡ (5)

(1) Asking for the number of spade controls.
(2) One spade control.
(3) Asking for heart controls.
(4) One heart control.
(5) Sign-off.

Knowing that the partnership was off two controls in spades and one control in hearts, responder knew that slam must be against the odds. Therefore he signed-off in 4 ♡ .

If The Opponents Interfere

1. If an opponent's bid over 2♢ is below the level of 3♢, then the 3♢ control asking bid is still on. If the interference is 3♢ or higher, then the control asking bid is off.

2. If an opponent bids four or five of a minor after responder's 3♢ bid, then the responses to the control asking bid are off. The new schedule of responses is:

Over four of a minor:

Pass	=A doubleton in the opponent's suit; minimum strength.
Double	=Three or four cards in the opponent's suit.
4♡	=A singleton in the opponent's suit; strength unknown.
4♠	=4-5-2-2 distribution; strength concentrated in the majors; maximum.
4 NT	=4-5-2-2 distribution; Qx or better in each minor; maximum.

A bid of the unbid minor = A void in the opponent's suit.

Over five of a minor:

Pass	=Minimum; a singleton or doubleton in the opponent's suit.
Double	=Three or four cards in the opponent's suit.
5♡	=A singleton in the opponent's suit; maximum strength.
5♠	=4-5-2-2 distribution; strength concentrated in the majors; maximum.
5 NT	=4-5-2-2 distribution; Qx or better in each minor; maximum strength.

A bid of the unbid minor = A void in the opponent's suit.

Opener can afford to force beyond game with a maximum because responder has announced slam interest by his 3 ◊ bid.

Interference Over 2 NT

> **Opener's Response after Opponent Overcalls with Three of a Minor over the 2 NT Inquiry Bid.**
>
> 3 ♡ = one card in opponent's suit.
> Pass = minimum hand (11-14) and two cards in opponent's suit.
> Double = three or four cards in opponent's suit.
> 3 ♠ = maximum (14-16); 4-5-2-2 with honor cards mostly in majors.
> 3 NT = maximum (14-16); 4-5-2-2 with Qx or better in both minors.
> Bidding the other minor shows a void in opponent's suit.

If an opponent overcalls in four or five of a minor, opener's rebids are analogous to his responses at the three level, allowing for a little more discretion due to the higher level.

Example 1.
                                  ♠ Q J x x
                                  ♡ K Q J x x
                                  ◊ x
                                  ♣ A x x

Opener	LHO	Responder	RHO
2 ◊	Pass	2 NT	3 ◊
3 ♡			

Example 2.
                                  ♠ K x x x
                                  ♡ A K x x x
                                  ◊ Q x
                                  ♣ x x

Opener	LHO	Responder	RHO
2 ◊	Pass	2 NT	3 ♣
Pass			

Example 3.
                                  ♠ K Q x x
                                  ♡ A Q J x x
                                  ◊ x x x
                                  ♣ x

Opener	LHO	Responder	RHO
2 ◊	Pass	2 NT	3 ◊
Double			

Example 4.
                                  ♠ K Q x x
                                  ♡ K Q x x x
                                  ◊ A x
                                  ♣ J x

Opener	LHO	Responder	RHO
2 ◊	Pass	2 NT	3 ♣
3 ♠			

Example 5.   ♠ A x x x
                         ♡ K Q x x x
                         ◊ K x
                         ♣ K x

Opener	LHO	Responder	RHO
2 ◊	Pass	2 NT	3 ♣
3 NT			

Example 6.   ♠ K J x x
                         ♡ A K x x x
                         ◊ Q x x x
                         ♣ —

Opener	LHO	Responder	RHO
2 ◊	Pass	2 NT	3 ♣
3 ◊			

**Responder's Rebid after Opponent Doubles Opener's
3 ♣ or 3 ◊ Response to a 2 NT Inquiry Bid.**

Responder's rebid of 4 ♣ is no longer a strength asking
bid as described in Chapter III. It now becomes a transfer
bid.

Transfer bids take over after an intervening double:

    4 ♣ transfers to 4 ♡
    4 ◊ transfers to 4 ♠

The transfer brings the lead into opener's hand to
protect the minor suit that was doubled.

Example 1.

♠ A J x x		♠ K Q x x	
♡ A J 10 x x		♡ Q x	
◇ K x x		◇ x x	
♣ x		♣ A K Q x x	

Opener	LHO	Responder	RHO
2 ◇	Pass	2 NT	Pass
3 ◇	Double	4 ◇ (1)	Pass
4 ♠	Pass	Pass	Pass

(1) Transfer to 4 ♠

Example 2

♠ J x x x		♠ K x	
♡ K Q 10 x x		♡ A J x x	
◇ x		◇ A Q J 10 x	
♣ A Q x		♣ x x	

Opener	LHO	Responder	RHO
2 ◇	Pass	2 NT	Pass
3 ♣	Double	4 ♣ (1)	Pass
4 ♡	Pass	Pass	Pass

(1) Transfer to 4 ♡. Not strength asking
after opponent's double.

Defense Against Flannery

Bidding After Opponent Opens 2 ◇

Double = at least a strong notrump.
2 ♡ = a takeout for spades, diamonds, and clubs.
2 ♠, 3 ♣ or 3 ◇ = natural overcall.
2 NT = takeout for the minors.

Occasionally I have seen different meanings assigned to these responses, but I believe the above responses to be the most flexible. Note that 2 NT is not used naturally, but is a distributional bid showing clubs and diamonds. With strong notrump hands, say double. This offers the greatest possibility of penalizing the opponents.

Examples:

	Opponent	You	Your Hand
1.	2 ◇	Double	♠ K 9 7
			♡ A 8
			◇ K Q 9 7 5
			♣ K 7 5
2.	2 ◇	2 ♡	♠ K 9 7 4
			♡ 5
			◇ A Q 7 4 2
			♣ A 10 6
3.	2 ◇	3 ◇	♠ Q 9
			♡ 8 6
			◇ A K J 9 4 3
			♣ Q 6 2
4.	2 ◇	2 NT	♠ Q 9
			♡ 8 6
			♡ A Q J 5 2
			♣ K J 10 6

Each of these hands are about the minimum you should have for the bid.

When opponents use 2 ♡ as Flannery instead of 2 ◇, Example 2 is the only one that changes. Examples 1, 3 and 4 remain the same. In Example 2, a 2 ♠ bid is for takeout.

In the fourth position the bids change:

Double = at least an opening bid. Partner may be able to pass for penalty.
2 NT = a strong notrump.
2♠, 3♣ or 3◇ = a natural overcall.
If 2◇ is passed out to fourth seat, 2♡ is a takeout, same as in second seat.

Examples

1. *Your Hand*
   ♠ A 6 5
   ♡ K 9
   ◇ K J 9 6
   ♣ Q 10 7 6

LHP	Partner	RHO	You
2◇	Pass	2♡ or 2♠	Double

2. *Your Hand*
   ♠ Q 9 3
   ♡ K 10
   ◇ A K 9
   ♣ A 10 8 7 5

LHO	Partner	RHO	You
2◇	Pass	2♡ or 2♠	2 NT

3. *Your Hand*
   ♠ K 8 4
   ♡ 9 4
   ◇ K 7
   ♣ A Q 10 8 6 4

LHO	Partner	RHO	You
2◇	Pass	2♡ or 2♠	3♣

This defensive structure is far from perfect; however it is the best that is currently available. It is difficult to defend against an opponent who opens a hand showing both major suits and an opening bid. If you have any suggestions please send them to me at:

Devyn Press
150 South Atlanta Street
32-L
Roswell, Georgia 30075

Does a 1♠ Response to a 1♡ Opening Require Five Spades?

When playing Flannery, if partner opens 1♡, he rarely has four spades. The only exceptions are when opener is strong enough to reverse with a 2♠ rebid, or when he has six or more hearts (My advice — never open Flannery with four spades and six hearts).

Accordingly, many players deem it unnecessary to respond 1♠ to a 1♡ opening without five or more spades. This treatment allows opener to raise spades with three-card support. On the following hand, after opening 1♡, opener can raise a 1♠ response to three:

Example 1.

♠ A x x
♡ A K x x x
♢ x x x
♣ A Q

In standard bidding, opener is required to have four spades to jump from the one level to the three level.

The disadvantage of requiring five or more spades for a 1♠ response is that the spade fit may be lost on hands such as the following, where opener has four spades and six hearts and is not strong enough to reverse.

Example B

Opener	Responder
♠ K x x x	♠ A Q x x
♡ A J x x x x	♡ x
◇ A x	◇ Q x x
♣ x	♣ x x x x x

Another problem with requiring five spades or more for a 1♠ response occurs when players use a 1 NT response to a 1♡ opening bid as forcing. For them it will be impossible to reach the right contract if they belong in 1 NT. This problem, along with several others, can be circumvented by playing The Forcing 1♠ Convention. In this convention the meanings of the 1♠ and the forcing 1 NT responses are reversed. By doing this the responder can bid 1♠ (meaning a forcing 1 NT) after a 1♡ opening. Opener can now bid 1 NT with a balanced hand.

Currently I suggest that the best treatment is for the 1♠ bid to tend to show five or more spades, and, if not, four spades to KJ10x or better. This allows opener to make a jump rebid of 3♠ on hands like Example A, knowing if partner has only four spades, the suit will be strong.

Regardless of what treatment you choose, it is important to discuss the sequence 1♡ - 1♠ with a new partner when you have agreed to play Flannery.

The following are examples of a 1♠ response after a 1♡ opening with only four spades:

1. ♠ K Q x x
   ♡ x x
   ◇ Q J x x
   ♣ x x x

2. ♠ A J x x
   ♡ x x
   ◇ Q x x x
   ♣ J x x

3. ♠ A K x x
   ♡ x x
   ◇ x x x x
   ♣ J x x

4. ♠ K J 10 x
   ♡ x x
   ◇ K x x x
   ♣ x x x

QUIZ TO CHAPTER IV

State the meaning of the last bid and whether it is forcing.

	Opener	*Opponent*	*Responder*	*Opponent*
1.	2 ◇ 3 ♡	Pass	2 NT	3 ♣
2.	2 ◇	2 ♠	3 ◇	
3.	2 ◇ Pass	Pass	2 NT	3 ◇
4.	2 ◇	Double		
5.	2 ◇ 3 ◇	Pass Double	2 NT 4 ♣	Pass
6.	2 ◇ 5 ♠	Pass	3 ◇	5 ♣
7.	2 ◇ 4 ♣	Pass	2 NT	3 ◇
8.	2 ◇ Double	Pass	2 NT	3 ♣
9.	2 ◇	2 NT		
10.	2 ◇	Pass	2 ♡	2 NT
11.	2 ◇ Pass	Pass	3 ◇	4 ◇

	Opener	*Opponent*	*Responder*	*Opponent*
12.	2 ◇ Double	Pass	3 ◇	4 ◇
13.	2 ◇	Pass	2 ♠	Double
14.	2 ◇ 4 ♡	Pass	2 NT	4 ♣
15.	2 ◇	2 ♡		
16.	2 ◇ 3 ♠	Pass	3 ◇	Pass
17.	2 ◇ 3 ♡	Pass Pass	3 ◇ 3 ♠	Pass
18.	2 ◇	2 ♠		
19.	2 ◇ 4 ♣	Pass	3 ◇	Pass
20.	2 ◇ 3 ♡ 4 ♣	Pass Pass	3 ◇ 3 ♠	Pass Pass

ANSWERS TO CHAPTER IV QUIZ

1. Not forcing. One card in opponent's suit.
2. Forcing. Control asking.
3. 4-5-2-2 minimum (11 to a poor 14 HCP).
4. Strong notrump.
5. Forcing. Transfer to 4 ♡.
6. 4-5-2-2 maximum (good 14 to 16 HCP); most strength in majors.
7. 4-5-0-4. Void in opponent's suit.
8. Three or four cards in opponent's suit.
9. Take-out for the minors.
10. Strong notrump in fourth seat.
11. 4-5-2-2 minimum (11 to a poor 14 HCP).
12. Three or four cards in opponent's suit.
13. Take-out; at least an opening bid. Partner may pass for penalty if he has spade strength.
14. Not forcing. One card in opponent's suit.
15. Take-out for spades, diamonds, and clubs.
16. Two spade controls.
17. Asking for heart controls.
18. At least a fair hand with five or more good spades.
19. No spade controls.
20. Two heart controls.

Chapter V

Opening Leads Against Flannery Auctions

Chapter V

Opening Leads Against
Flannery Auctions

When the opponents open the bidding with a Flannery
2 ◇ bid and eventually settle in a major suit contract, there
are several plans of attack to be considered. In order of
importance, they are:
1. Leading trump to minimize declarer's ruffing values;
2. Cashing and establishing winners, especially in the
   minors, and waiting for winners that cannot go
   away, especially in the majors;
3. "Tapping" the long trump hand, that is, forcing it
   to ruff, in order to establish your own small trumps;
4. Playing for ruffs and overruffs, by yourself or
   partner;
5. Defending passively — looking for safe leads that
   give nothing away and waiting for tricks.
Leading trump is frequently the best defense against
Flannery auctions. It is especially effective when declarer
is playing a seven or eight card fit, as two or three trump
leads will nullify, or greatly reduce, opportunities for
ruffing — the principal advantage declarer hoped to gain
by playing in a suit contract.

On the other end of the spectrum, totally passive
defense is seldom effective against Flannery auctions.
Passive defense gives declarer two opportunities to
succeed: to make tricks by ruffing, or to establish long suit
tricks for discards. It is usually better to attack, hoping to
establish winners, or to lead trump, hoping to nullify
ruffing values, than to place safety above all other considerations. A "safe" lead that does not cost a trick, will
often cost a tempo and the contract.

Nevertheless, each of the five defensive plans listed above — leading trump, cashing winners, tapping, ruffing and passivity — will be the right defense on some hands. Still other hands will require a combination of defensive plans, such as first cashing certain winners that might be discarded, and then playing trump to prevent ruffs.

Choosing the right defensive plan is based on two considerations; your own hand, and the opponent's auction, which will often reveal the best defense.

For example, listen to the following auction:

North	South
2 ◇	2 NT
3 ♣	3 ♡
4 ♡	Pass

The following points are clear:

1. North has 4-5-1-3 distribution.
2. South has about 9-11 HCP, possibly 12 HCP, with wasted diamond values opposite North's singleton.
3. North has a good hand, 14 or more HCP.
4. South probably has three hearts (two or four are possible, but against the odds).
5. A trump lead should probably be effective.

In contrast, listen to the following auction:

North	South
2 ◇	2 ♠
Pass	

Here, South's hand is poorly defined, but the following information is available:

1. South has more spades than hearts.
2. South probably has 9 HCP or less, but could have as

many as 11 HCP with a poor fit (three small spades and a singleton or void in hearts).

3. South may have a five card minor, perhaps a six card minor (unlikely in diamonds, as South might have passed 2 ◇).

4. North may have a strong hand (only exceptional hands justify further action after a sign-off).

In this example, a trump lead should be given strong consideration.

Rather than attempt to catalogue every possible auction, the remainder of this chapter is presented in a quiz format. You have been given the same six hands to lead from in each problem.

(A)   ♠ K 10 9 2   (B)   ♠ A 4
        ♡ J 3   ♡ A 10 2
        ◇ 10 8 6   ◇ J 9 4 3
        ♣ K Q J 7   ♣ 8 7 6 2

(C)   ♠ K 2   (D)   ♠ 8 3 2
        ♡ A Q 7   ♡ 10 6 4
        ◇ 8 4 3 2   ◇ J 8 3 2
        ♣ J 9 3 2   ♣ A J 7

(E)   ♠ Q 9 2   (F)   ♠ 8
        ♡ A J 2   ♡ K 3 2
        ◇ K Q 6 2   ◇ J 6 5 3
        ♣ 7 5 2   ♣ 10 8 6 4 2

In each case, choose what you would lead from each of the above six hands on each of the following auctions. Of course, the right lead will vary, depending on the auction.

	North	South			North	South
I.	2 ◇	4 ♡		II.	2 ◇	4 ◇ (1)
	Pass				4 ♠	Pass
					(1) transfer to spades	

	North	South			North	South
III.	2 ◇	2 ♡		IV.	2 ◇	2 NT
	Pass				3 ♣	3 ♠

	North	South			North	South
V.	2 ◇	2 NT		VI.	2 ◇	2 NT
	4 ◇	4 ♡			3 ♡	4 ♠

The answers and reasoning behind them start on the next page.

Answers to Quiz

AUCTION I.   *North*   *South*
             2♦   4♡
             Pass

A.   Club king. Declarer has power to spare, and per-
      haps, four trumps opposite dummy's five. Cash out.
B.   Spade ace, followed by another spade, hoping part-
      ner has a quick entry to give you a spade ruff or a
      trump promotion.
C.   A passive diamond is your best chance. If declarer
      attempts to ruff spades in hand, he will be jolted by
      your overruff. The spade king could also succeed,
      but if partner has the ace, you will get another
      chance.
D.   Heart four. With no attractive alternative, hope
      that a trump lead will leave declarer one ruff short.
E.   Diamond king. Plan two — cash tricks in minors, if
      possible, and wait for major suit winners.
F.   Spade eight. If your heart king is an entry, you
      should be able to reach partner's hand for a spade
      ruff.

AUCTION II.   *North*   *South*
              2♦   4♦ (1)
              4♠   Pass
              (1) transfer to spades

A.   Club king. You plan to lead clubs at every opportun-
      ity to force declarer to ruff. You may end up with
      control of the trump suit by "tapping" declarer.
B.   Spade ace, followed by another spade, hoping to kill
      ruffs.
C.   A small diamond. Auctions such as this, where

declarer has power to spare, often require aggressive defense. On this hand your honors are favorably placed, and defensive prospects are bright for a passive defense. Either a club or a diamond lead might be best, but the diamond is safer.

D. Spade two. "If in doubt, lead trump." The club ace is an attractive alternative, with hopes to cash minor suit tricks that might go away. If you lead the club ace, you can decide from partner's play and dummy's hand whether to try diamonds or continue clubs.

E. Diamond king. Cash winners and wait for more.

F. Club four. A diamond lead could work out better but is more dangerous for two reasons: your diamonds are shorter; and they are headed by the jack.

AUCTION III.

North	South
2 ◇	2 ♡
Pass	

A. Heart jack. Declarer may be in a poor trump fit. Protect your spade honors with trump leads. The club tricks can probably wait. Still, who could blame you too much if you lead the club king (except partner, of course)?

B. Several good possibilities: the heart two, to stop ruffs (this is better than the ace, followed by the deuce, since if partner holds only two hearts, he would not have one to return when he is on lead). Alternatively, lead a minor. If declarer ruffs spades in the short hand, you will overruff.

C. A diamond. Overruffs coming. See B.

D. Heart four. With no attractive alternative, lead trump, kill ruffs.

E. Diamond king. Cash and wait.

F. Spade eight. Play for ruffs.

AUCTION IV.　　*North*　　*South*
　　　　　　　　2♦　　　　2 NT
　　　　　　　　3♣　　　　3♠

A.　Club king. Establish club tricks, wait for spade tricks. A tapping game may also develop.
B.　Club eight, through dummy's suit.
C.　Club two, dummy's long suit. The lead of the spade king could be brilliant, but risks dropping a crucial trick on a hand in which declarer has no strength to spare.
D.　Spade two. "If in doubt, ..."
E.　Club seven. It is pointless to lead the diamond king, dummy's singleton suit.
F.　Club four. You have to lead something.

AUCTION V.　　*North*　　*South*
　　　　　　　　2♦　　　　2 NT
　　　　　　　　4♦　　　　4♡

A.　Heart jack. Finally an auction in which the club king from K Q J 7 is not right. Dummy is void. Might as well start trump.
B.　Heart two, or ace and another heart.
C.　Spade king, playing for overruffs. Alternately, a diamond lead.
D.　Heart four, to cut down on ruffs.
E.　Diamond king. Cash tricks. If declarer plays for a crossruff, you may come to two trump tricks.
F.　Spade eight. Partner should have entries for your ruff.

AUCTION VI.   *North*   *South*
                2 ♢   2 NT
                3 ♡   4 ♠

A. Club king. Dummy is 4-5-2-2 minimum. Declarer's strength is not limited. Cashing minor suit winners on 4-5-2-2 hands is often best before tricks disappear.
B. Club eight. Safer than a diamond attack.
C. A diamond. Although your heart holding is poorly placed, hope to develop fast winners.
D. Diamond two. With exactly two diamonds in dummy, it is relatively safe to lead from the jack. It doesn't cost when partner has, for example, Qxxx. While there is still some danger in a diamond lead, it will be necessary for partner to lead clubs through.
E. Diamond king. Cash and wait.
F. Diamond three. As noted in D, the lead from a jack is safer when dummy has precisely two cards in the suit. A club lead is at least as dangerous on this auction.

Chapter VI

Summary of Flannery and Hands from Actual Play

Chapter VI

Summary of Flannery

1. An opening bid of 2 ♢ shows exactly four spades and five hearts and ordinary opening strength of 11 to 16 HCP. Distribution points are not counted when opening 2 ♢ .

2. A hand which is worth a reverse (a 1 ♡ opening followed by a rebid of 2 ♠) is too strong to open 2 ♢ . A good 16 HCP hand containing strong suits and a singleton or void should be opened 1 ♡ .

Example:

♠ A K Q x
♡ K Q J x x
♢ J x x
♣ x

With 17 or 18 HCP, open 1 ♡ and over a 1 NT response by partner, rebid 2 ♠ which is not forcing.

With 19 or 20 HCP, open 1 ♡ and rebid 3 ♠, which is forcing to game.

3. 11 HCP hands should contain 2½ defensive tricks or exceptionally strong suits to qualify as an opening bid.

4. Responses of 2 ♡ and 2 ♠ are to play and should be passed except with a maximum hand containing a singleton or void. If opener does bid after a sign-off of 2 ♡ or 2 ♠, he bids his longer minor as a game try.

5. A 3 ♣ response is also a sign-off bid. Opener should consider raising to 4 ♣ with maximum values and at least three clubs.

6. Responses of 3 ♡ and 3 ♠ are game tries — 9 to 11 HCP and at least four card trump support with honor cards in both minors — asking opener to bid game if he

has maximum values.

7. A 4♣ response is a transfer to 4♡. A 4♢ response is a transfer to 4♠. Responder may simply bid 4♡ or 4♠ directly over a 2♢ opening bid if he has tenaces in the minors and wants the lead coming into his hand.

8. 3♢ is a special bid. It asks opener about controls in the major suits, starting with spades. Ace, king, and queen are controls. The next bid, either a suit or notrump bid, over opener's response asks about heart controls.

Controls are shown in the following manner. One step shows one control, two steps, two controls, etc. The fourth step shows no controls.

Opener		Responder
2♢		3♢ (asks about spade
3♡	= one control	controls)
3♠	= two controls	
3 NT	= three controls	
4♣	= no controls	

9. A 2 NT response shows at least game interest and asks opener to describe his hand. He rebids as follows:

3♣ or 3♢ = three cards in the bid suit; HCP unknown.

3♡ = minimum hand with two cards in each minor (4-5-2-2).

3♠ = maximum with most strength in majors (4-5-2-2).

3 NT = maximum with at least Qx or better in each minor (4-5-2-2).

4♣ or 4♢ = four cards in the bid suit; 4-5-0-4 or 4-5-4-0; HCP unknown.

10. After the auction

Opener	Responder
2 ◇	2 NT
3 ♣ or 3 ◇	

a 3 ♡ or 3 ♠ bid by responder is nonforcing but does invite opener to bid a game with maximal values (a good 14-16 HCP).

11. After the auction

Opener	Responder
2 ◇	2 NT
3 ♣ or 3 ◇	

a 4 ♣ bid by responder is strength asking. Opener bids 4 ◇ with a minimum or 4 ♡ with a maximum.

If an opponent doubles a 3 ♣ or 3 ◇ rebid the strength asking 4 ♣ is off. In this case 4 ♣ is a transfer bid to 4 ♡ and 4 ◇ is a transfer bid to 4 ♠. This structure allows opener to become the declarer so that the opening lead will come up to, rather than through, his hand.

12. After the auction

Opener	Responder
2 ◇	2 NT

if an opponent bids 3 ♣ or 3 ◇, opener rebids as follows:

Pass = a minimum 4-5-2-2.
Double = three or four cards in the opponents's suit.
3 ♡ = one card in the opponent's suit.
3 ♠ = a maximum 4-5-2-2, with strength concentrated in the majors.
3 NT = a maximum 4-5-2-2, with Qx or better in

both minors.

Bidding the other minor = a void in opponent's suit.

If an opponent bids four or five of a minor, opener's rebids are analogous to his rebids when the overcall was at the three level . . . taking into account the increased level.

13. When an opponent overcalls four or five of a minor over 3 ◊, the control asking bid is off. Opener responds the same as over interference to a 2 NT, only one step higher.

After the auction

Opener	Responder
2 ◊	3 ◊

if an opponent bids four of five of a minor, opener rebids as follows:

Pass = a minimum 4-5-2-2.

Double = three or four cards in the opponent's suit.

4 ♡ = one card in the opponent's suit.

4 ♠ = a maximum 4-5-2-2, with strength concentrated in the majors.

4 NT = a maximum 4-5-2-2, with Qx or better in both minors.

Bidding the other minor = a void in opponent's suit.

14. Responder counts distribution points as follows:

	Doubleton	Singleton	Void
Four card support	1	3	5
Three card support	1	2	3

Flannery Hands from Actual Play

The following hands from club games to international competition show Flannery hands as they were actually bid, or occasionally, misbid. Where possible both the result of the hand and the number of IMPs or match points won are included. The results have not been changed.

Two changes have been made in the hands that follow. First, the table directions have been changed for convenience so that the Flannery hands are North-South (except where the auction is shown at both tables of a team game). Second, the auction on hands 22 and 23 has been altered, so that the new method of responding in competition is shown. The final result is not affected in either case, and these changes will avoid confusion. For ease of reference, the hands are loosely grouped into the following themes:

Deal Subject

1-19 Sign-Off Bids
20-21 Game Tries
22-32 The 2 NT Asking Bid
33-44 Competitive Auctions
45-46 The 3 ◊ Control Asking Bid
47-50 Transfer Bids
51-62 Team Hands

Readers may think the hands have been stacked to show only the good results and that the bad results have been left out. The simple truth is that Flannery is so accurate and easy to use that there is rarely any serious difficulty in bidding a hand. These rare hands that do cause trouble are usually even more difficult to bid if you are not using Flannery.

1

LANCASTER REGIONAL, 1983
MEN'S PAIRS

DEALER: North
VULNERABLE: Both
CONTRACT: 2 ♦
DECLARER: North
NORTH-SOUTH SCORE: +110
TOP ON BOARD: 12
NORTH-SOUTH MATCHPOINTS: 9½
OPENING LEAD: ♠ J

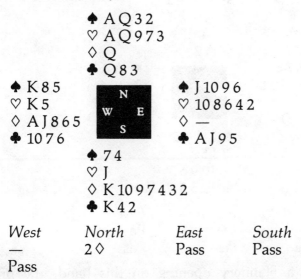

```
              ♠ A Q 3 2
              ♡ A Q 9 7 3
              ◊ Q
              ♣ Q 8 3
  ♠ K 8 5                    ♠ J 10 9 6
  ♡ K 5          N           ♡ 10 8 6 4 2
  ◊ A J 8 6 5  W   E         ◊ —
  ♣ 10 7 6       S           ♣ A J 9 5
              ♠ 7 4
              ♡ J
              ◊ K 10 9 7 4 3 2
              ♣ K 4 2
```

West	North	East	South
—	2 ◊	Pass	Pass
Pass			

Here is another unexpected dividend from Flannery. North and South could stop conveniently in 2 ◊ on this misfit.

Pairs who play 1 NT forcing after a 1 ♡ opening may also arrive at 2 ◊. However the hand is played better from the North where tenaces are protected. On this hand East is endplayed on the opening lead. Any lead helps declarer play the hand.

2

DEALER: North
VULNERABLE: Both
CONTRACT: 2♠
DECLARER: South
NORTH-SOUTH SCORE: +140
TOP ON BOARD: 12
NORTH-SOUTH MATCHPOINTS: 9
OPENING LEAD: ♠7

```
                    ♠ K 10 4 2
                    ♡ A K 7 4 3
                    ◇ J 4
                    ♣ A 2
        ♠ 7 6                         ♠ A 8 3
        ♡ Q 9 8 2        N            ♡ 10 6
        ◇ A K 8 5    W       E        ◇ Q 7 2
        ♣ Q 9 5          S            ♣ K J 7 6 4
                    ♠ Q J 9 5
                    ♡ J 5
                    ◇ 10 9 6 3
                    ♣ 10 8 3
```

West	North	East	South
—	2◇	Pass	2♠
Pass	Pass	Pass	

After a Flannery opening on this hand, the proper
contract of 2♠ was reached, making three.

At those tables where North opened 1♡ and the hand
was passed out, North-South took seven tricks.

The West player who balanced with 1 NT received a top
score. After a heart lead he was able to make four. When
North got in with the ace of clubs he tried to cash hearts,
setting up the tenth trick for declarer.

3

PITTSBURGH CLUB GAME, 1984

DEALER: West
VULNERABLE: East-West
CONTRACT: 2♠
DECLARER: South
NORTH-SOUTH SCORE: +140
TOP ON BOARD: 8
NORTH-SOUTH MATCHPOINTS: 7
OPENING LEAD: ◊9

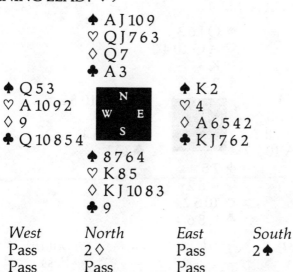

```
                    ♠ A J 10 9
                    ♡ Q J 7 6 3
                    ◊ Q 7
                    ♣ A 3
  ♠ Q 5 3                         ♠ K 2
  ♡ A 10 9 2          N          ♡ 4
  ◊ 9             W       E       ◊ A 6 5 4 2
  ♣ Q 10 8 5 4        S          ♣ K J 7 6 2
                    ♠ 8 7 6 4
                    ♡ K 8 5
                    ◊ K J 10 8 3
                    ♣ 9
```

West	North	East	South
Pass	2◊	Pass	2♠
Pass	Pass	Pass	

East's first pass is reasonable, but when South signs off at 2♠, East should reopen the auction with 2 NT, asking West to choose his longer minor. East-West can make 4♣.

When vulnerable it is a good idea to be careful when entering the auction over a Flannery opening bid, but don't be afraid to do so. East let North-South steal the contract. With a slip in the defense, declarer made 3♠, but making two would have been the same match point result.

4

DEALER: South
VULNERABLE: North-South
CONTRACT: 2♡
DECLARER: South
NORTH-SOUTH SCORE: −100
TOP ON BOARD: 12
NORTH-SOUTH MATCHPOINTS: 10
OPENING LEAD ♡ 9

```
                    ♠ Q J 6 3
                    ♡ A Q 10 4 3
                    ◇ K 3
                    ♣ 9 5
    ♠ 9 4                             ♠ A K 10 8 2
    ♡ 9 7 5          N                ♡ J 6
    ◇ A J 8 7      W   E              ◇ Q 9 6 4
    ♣ A 10 7 2       S               ♣ Q J
                    ♠ 7 5
                    ♡ K 8 2
                    ◇ 10 5 2
                    ♣ K 8 6 4 3
```

West	North	East	South
—	—	—	Pass
Pass	2◇	Pass	2♡
Pass	Pass	Pass	

The North players who opened the hand 1♡ gave East the opportunity to overcall 1♠, enabling the East-West pairs to bid to 2♠, making three, or 3◇, making four.

The Flannery opening bid kept East-West out of the auction. North-South played in 2♡, down one, for a near top.

5

PITTSBURGH CLUB GAME, 1982

DEALER: North
VULNERABLE: Both
CONTRACT: 2♠
DECLARER: South
NORTH-SOUTH SCORE: −100
TOP ON BOARD: 12
NORTH-SOUTH MATCHPOINTS: 12
OPENING LEAD: ♣K

```
                    ♠ K 7 3 2
                    ♡ A K Q 10 4
                    ◇ 5
                    ♣ Q 10 5
    ♠ Q 10                         ♠ A 8
    ♡ 7 5 3 2         N            ♡ 9
    ◇ K 9 7 2      W     E         ◇ A J 8 4 3
    ♣ A K J          S            ♣ 9 7 6 3 2
                    ♠ J 9 6 5 4
                    ♡ J 8 6
                    ◇ Q 10 6
                    ♣ 8 4
```

West	North	East	South
—	2◇	Pass	2♠
Pass	Pass	Pass	

East-West got a zero on this board when North-South played 2♠ after a Flannery opening.

When the 2♠ bid was passed around to East, he felt that West probably had a heart stack and also could have three or four spades, so he chose to pass. He could have been right, but timidity rarely pays big dividends at the bridge table and he should have bid 2 NT as a takeout for the minors. A re-opening double would show a more balanced hand.

East-West can make 4◇.

6

SPRING NATIONALS, 1984
CHARITY GAME

DEALER: North
VULNERABLE: Neither
CONTRACT: 2♡
DECLARER: South
NORTH-SOUTH SCORE: +170
TOP ON BOARD: 12
NORTH-SOUTH MATCHPOINTS: 10
OPENING LEAD: ♡5

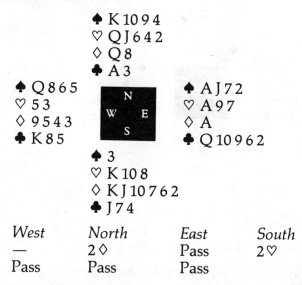

```
                    ♠ K 10 9 4
                    ♡ Q J 6 4 2
                    ◊ Q 8
                    ♣ A 3
    ♠ Q 8 6 5                      ♠ A J 7 2
    ♡ 5 3          N               ♡ A 9 7
    ◊ 9 5 4 3    W   E             ◊ A
    ♣ K 8 5        S               ♣ Q 10 9 6 2
                    ♠ 3
                    ♡ K 10 8
                    ◊ K J 10 7 6 2
                    ♣ J 7 4
```

West	North	East	South
—	2◊	Pass	2♡
Pass	Pass	Pass	

Against this contract it was wrong to lead a heart and continue hearts. Declarer won the second heart and drove out the ace of diamonds and was now able to take ten tricks. The majority of times it is right to lead trump against a Flannery contract, but not all the time.

DAYTON REGIONAL, 1984
MEN'S AND WOMEN'S PAIRS

DEALER: West
VULNERABLE: Both
CONTRACT: 2♠
DECLARER: South
NORTH-SOUTH SCORE: +110
TOP ON BOARD: Men's Pairs - 17. Women's Pairs - 12.
NORTH-SOUTH MATCHPOINTS: Men's Pairs - 14½.
    Women's Pairs - 9.
OPENING LEAD: ♣K

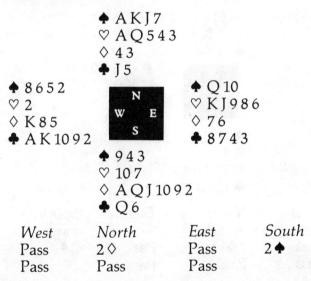

```
              ♠ A K J 7
              ♡ A Q 5 4 3
              ◇ 4 3
              ♣ J 5
  ♠ 8 6 5 2              ♠ Q 10
  ♡ 2           N        ♡ K J 9 8 6
  ◇ K 8 5    W     E     ◇ 7 6
  ♣ A K 10 9 2  S        ♣ 8 7 4 3
              ♠ 9 4 3
              ♡ 10 7
              ◇ A Q J 10 9 2
              ♣ Q 6
```

West	North	East	South
Pass	2◇	Pass	2♠
Pass	Pass	Pass	

This hand illustrates another advantage in playing Flannery. With poor major suit cards and all his strength in the minors, South knows to sign off in 2♠.

Playing IMPS, 2◇ should be passed with such a good suit, but at matchpoints, the decision is close.

Pairs who opened this hand with 1♠ or 1♡ ended up going down at the three or four level.

8

DAYTON REGIONAL, 1984
OPEN PAIRS

DEALER: South
VULNERABLE: North-South
CONTRACT: 2♠
DECLARER: South
NORTH-SOUTH SCORE: +110
TOP ON BOARD: 12
NORTH-SOUTH MATCHPOINTS: 8½
OPENING LEAD: ◊ J

```
                    ♠ J 10 8 3
                    ♡ 10 8 7 5 2
                    ◊ A K
                    ♣ A 8
        ♠ K 9                       ♠ Q 6 4 2
        ♡ A Q 6         N           ♡ K 9 4 3
        ◊ J 10 8 3   W     E        ◊ 7 5
        ♣ J 7 6 4       S           ♣ K 9 3
                    ♠ A 7 5
                    ♡ J
                    ◊ Q 9 6 4 2
                    ♣ Q 10 5 2
```

West	North	East	South
—	—	—	Pass
Pass	2◊	Pass	2♠
Pass	Pass	Pass	

South has a routine 2♠ call after North opens 2◊, since game must be out of reach. Pairs not using Flannery usually played 1 NT, going down. 2♠ made, but would surely have been set if West had led the spade king.

Trump leads are often effective against Flannery auctions and should always be considered.

9

DEALER: West
VULNERABLE: North-South
CONTRACT: 2♡
DECLARER: South
NORTH-SOUTH SCORE: +140
TOP ON BOARD: 12
NORTH-SOUTH MATCHPOINTS: 9
OPENING LEAD: ◇5

```
                    ♠ K 8 6 5
                    ♡ A J 9 8 5
                    ◇ K 9
                    ♣ K 4
    ♠ Q 4 3                         ♠ J 10 9 7
    ♡ K Q 10 4 3        N           ♡ —
    ◇ Q 6 5         W       E       ◇ A J 10 4 3
    ♣ J 7              S            ♣ Q 9 8 6
                    ♠ A 2
                    ♡ 7 6 2
                    ◇ 8 7 2
                    ♣ A 10 5 3 2
```

West	North	East	South
Pass	2◇	Pass	2♡
Pass	Pass	Pass	

My partner and I were able to stop in 2♡ while most of
the North-South pairs played in higher contracts. It takes
careful play and timing to come to nine tricks. We took
two clubs, two spades, a spade ruff and four heart tricks.

One pair made 4♡ and I still can't figure out where they
got their tenth trick.

10

SPRING NATIONALS, 1984

DEALER: North
VULNERABLE: East-West
CONTRACT: 3♣
DECLARER: South
NORTH-SOUTH SCORE: +130
TOP ON BOARD: 12
NORTH-SOUTH MATCHPOINTS: 3½
OPENING LEAD: ♣2

```
                   ♠ Q J 8 4
                   ♡ A Q J 9 6
                   ◇ 10
                   ♣ A 8 4
  ♠ A 5 3                          ♠ K 9 6 2
  ♡ 10 5 4          N             ♡ K 8 2
  ◇ K J 9 4 3    W     E          ◇ Q 7 6 2
  ♣ 5 2             S             ♣ 10 9
                   ♠ 10 7
                   ♡ 7 3
                   ◇ A 8 5
                   ♣ K Q J 7 6 3
```

West	North	East	South
—	2◇	Pass	3♣ (1)
Pass	Pass	Pass	

(1) Sign-off

   In my opinion this hand is too good to make a sign-off bid. If opener has a maximum hand there can easily be a good play for game. I would have responded 2 NT with the South hand. Opener would have bid 3♣ and I would have raised to five. With the North hand concealed, declarer wins the opening lead by East, either a club or diamond, and, at trick two leads the ten of spades. If West doesn't rise with the ace and shift to a heart, 5 ◇ cannot be beaten.

11

DEALER: North
VULNERABLE: East-West
CONTRACT: 2♠
DECLARER: South
NORTH-SOUTH: +110
TOP ON BOARD: 12
NORTH-SOUTH MATCHPOINTS: 9½
OPENING LEAD: ♠2

```
                    ♠ A 10 9 4
                    ♡ A K 10 7 3
                    ◇ 9 7
                    ♣ J 8
   ♠ K J 3 2                        ♠ 6 5
   ♡ 8              ┌─────────┐     ♡ Q J 9 5 4
   ◇ K J 10 8 5 2   │    N    │     ◇ A Q 6
   ♣ 3 2            │  W   E  │     ♣ Q 10 9
                    │    S    │
                    └─────────┘
                    ♠ Q 8 7
                    ♡ 6 2
                    ◇ 4 3
                    ♣ A K 7 6 5 4
```

West	North	East	South
—	2◇	Pass	2♠
Pass	Pass	Pass	

After a Flannery opening, North-South were able to stop in 2♠.

Most East-West pairs played in 3◇, making. In the above auction, if West stretches and bids 3◇ over 2♠, East is under considerable pressure. If he chooses to bid, South will double.

12

**MYRTLE BEACH REGIONAL, 1984
OPEN PAIRS FINAL**

DEALER: North
VULNERABLE: North-South
CONTRACT: 2♡
DECLARER: South
NORTH-SOUTH SCORE: +110
TOP ON BOARD: 25
NORTH-SOUTH MATCHPOINTS: 20
OPENING LEAD: ◊ Q

```
                    ♠ K Q 10 6
                    ♡ Q 10 8 3 2
                    ◊ A 10 8
                    ♣ 9
     ♠ J 3                          ♠ 9 8 7 2
     ♡ K 7 5          N             ♡ A 6
     ◊ Q J 9 5     W     E          ◊ K 7 4
     ♣ Q 8 5 3        S             ♣ A J 4 2
                    ♠ A 5 4
                    ♡ J 9 4
                    ◊ 6 3 2
                    ♣ K 10 7 6
```

West	North	East	South
—	2 ◊	Pass	2 ♡
Pass	Pass	Pass	

Many pairs not using Flannery played 2♠ or 1 NT.
Those using Flannery played 2♡, making two.

13

PITTSBURGH CLUB GAME, 1979

DEALER: North
VULNERABLE: Neither
CONTRACT: 2♠
DECLARER: South
NORTH-SOUTH SCORE: +140
TOP ON BOARD: 8
NORTH-SOUTH MATCHPOINTS: 8
OPENING LEAD: ♡9

```
                    ♠ A 10 8 3
                    ♡ K Q 10 5 2
                    ◇ 8 7
                    ♣ A 2
      ♠ K 9 6 4          N          ♠ Q 7
      ♡ 9            W       E       ♡ A J 8 7 6
      ◇ K J 10 5 4 2       S        ◇ Q 3
      ♣ 6 4                          ♣ Q 10 8 7
                    ♠ J 5 2
                    ♡ 4 3
                    ◇ A 9 6
                    ♣ K J 9 5 3
```

West	North	East	South
—	2◇	Pass	2♠
Pass	Pass	Pass	

Only two North-South pairs achieved a plus score on this hand.

One pair played in 2♡ making two. The other pair, playing Flannery, reached 2♠, making three for a top board (with the aid of a helpful defense).

The rest of the North-South pairs played in either 1 NT or 2♡, down after North opened with 1♡.

14

DEALER: West
VULNERABLE: North-South
CONTRACT: 2♡
DECLARER: South
NORTH-SOUTH: +110
TOP ON BOARD: 8
NORTH-SOUTH MATCHPOINTS: 7
OPENING LEAD: ♡5

```
                    ♠ A K 9 4
                    ♡ A 6 4 3 2
                    ◇ 9 6 3
                    ♣ A
        ♠ 7 5 2              ♠ J 10 6 3
        ♡ 5                  ♡ K Q J 9
        ◇ A Q 8 5 2          ◇ K J 4
        ♣ Q 8 6 5            ♣ 7 3
                    ♠ Q 8
                    ♡ 10 8 7
                    ◇ 10 7
                    ♣ K J 10 9 4 2
```

West	North	East	South
Pass	2◇	Pass	2♡
Pass	Pass	Pass	

West led a trump to hold the contract to two.

Most of the field was in 3♡ or 4♡ doubled.

If North had held Axx in one minor and a small singleton in the other, his maximum would justify a game try. He would have bid three of his long minor.

I recommend that you never make an uninvited game try when you hold three small in a minor, regardless of how good your hand is.

15

COLUMBUS REGIONAL, 1984
OPEN PAIRS

DEALER: North
VULNERABLE: North-South
CONTRACT: 2♠
DECLARER: South
NORTH-SOUTH SCORE: +140
TOP ON BOARD: 12
NORTH-SOUTH MATCHPOINTS: 11
OPENING LEAD: ♠10

```
                    ♠ A K J 4
                    ♡ K J 9 5 2
                    ◇ Q 7
                    ♣ 8 3
      ♠ 10 9 5              ♠ 8 6 3
      ♡ 8 3          N      ♡ Q 10 7 6
      ◇ K 8 4 3    W   E    ◇ A 10 5 2
      ♣ 7 6 5 4      S      ♣ A K
                    ♠ Q 7 2
                    ♡ A 4
                    ◇ J 9 6
                    ♣ Q J 10 9 2
```

West	North	East	South
—	2◇	Pass	2♠
Pass	Pass	Pass	

Most of the field played 3 NT, down one or two. A few were in 2 NT making.

After a Flannery opening, South responded 2♠, holding three to an honor, making three.

It is usually better to play the 4-3 spade fit, holding a spade honor, rather than the 5-2 heart fit, as the hand with three spades can ruff heart losers.

YOUNGSTOWN SECTIONAL, 1980
MEN'S PAIR

DEALER: West
VULNERABLE: East-West
CONTRACT: 3♣
DECLARER: South
NORTH-SOUTH SCORE: +110
TOP ON BOARD: 8
NORTH-SOUTH MATCHPOINTS: 7½
OPENING LEAD: ◇ 4

```
                    ♠ Q 6 5 2
                    ♡ A K 10 5 4
                    ◇ K 9 6
                    ♣ 4
    ♠ K 9 8                        ♠ A J 10 7 4
    ♡ Q 9 6 2          N           ♡ J 7
    ◇ J 5 4        W       E       ◇ Q 10 8 3
    ♣ A 8 5            S           ♣ K 10
                    ♠ 3
                    ♡ 8 3
                    ◇ A 7 2
                    ♣ Q J 9 7 6 3 2
```

West	North	East	South
Pass	2◇	Pass	3♣ (1)
Pass	Pass	Pass	

(1) Sign-off

After North's Flannery opening, East-West were unable to find their spade fit. The two North-South pairs who were playing Flannery bought the contract for 3♣, making, and tied for top.

At those tables where North opened 1♡, East overcalled 1♠, and East-West played the hand in 2 or 3♠, making three.

17

DEALER: North
VULNERABLE: East-West
CONTRACT: 4♡
DECLARER: South
NORTH-SOUTH SCORE: −100
TOP ON BOARD: 12
NORTH-SOUTH MATCHPOINTS: 10
OPENING LEAD: ♣K

```
                    ♠ Q J 7 5
                    ♡ A K Q 9 2
                    ◇ Q 7 2
                    ♣ 6
  ♠ K 4 3                              ♠ A 10 9 8 6
  ♡ 7 4            ┌─────────┐        ♡ J 5
  ◇ J 10 4         │    N    │        ◇ A K 3
  ♣ A K Q 10 5     │  W   E  │        ♣ 9 3 2
                   │    S    │
                   └─────────┘
                    ♠ 2
                    ♡ 10 8 6 3
                    ◇ 9 8 6 5
                    ♣ J 8 7 4
```

West	North	East	South
—	2◇	Pass	4♡ (1)
Pass	Pass	Pass	

(1) Sign-off

After a Flannery 2◇ opening by North, South jumped to 4♡. He knew the hand belonged to East-West and took a premature sacrifice. With the points evenly distributed between the East-West hands, neither was able to double.

Declarer went down two while the opponents were cold for 4♠. North-South got a near top.

18

SPRING NATIONALS, 1984
CHARITY GAME

DEALER: West
VULNERABLE: East-West
CONTRACT: 4♡
DECLARER: South
NORTH-SOUTH SCORE: −50
TOP ON BOARD: 12
NORTH-SOUTH MATCHPOINTS: 4
OPENING LEAD: ♡4

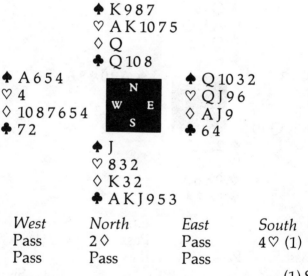

```
                    ♠ K 9 8 7
                    ♡ A K 10 7 5
                    ◊ Q
                    ♣ Q 10 8
      ♠ A 6 5 4                      ♠ Q 10 3 2
      ♡ 4              N             ♡ Q J 9 6
      ◊ 10 8 7 6 5 4  W   E         ◊ A J 9
      ♣ 7 2              S           ♣ 6 4
                    ♠ J
                    ♡ 8 3 2
                    ◊ K 3 2
                    ♣ A K J 9 5 3
```

West	North	East	South
Pass	2◊	Pass	4♡ (1)
Pass	Pass	Pass	

(1) Sign-off

South, with no major suit fit, is not interested in a slam, so he bids 4♡ directly. He wants the lead coming up to his hand to protect minor suit holdings.

This hand must be played very carefully. South must ruff two spades or duck a trump to maintain control to go down only one. You can see that there are nine tricks at 3 NT, but in the long run the 4♡ bid by South will work out best.

19

DEALER: West
VULNERABLE: East-West
CONTRACT: 4♡
DECLARER: South
NORTH-SOUTH SCORE: +420
TOP ON BOARD: 12
NORTH-SOUTH MATCHPOINTS: 11
OPENING LEAD: ♡9

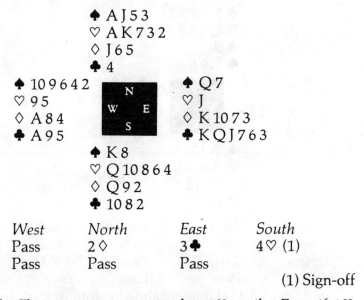

```
              ♠ A J 5 3
              ♡ A K 7 3 2
              ◇ J 6 5
              ♣ 4
♠ 10 9 6 4 2      N        ♠ Q 7
♡ 9 5          W     E     ♡ J
◇ A 8 4           S        ◇ K 10 7 3
♣ A 9 5                    ♣ K Q J 7 6 3
              ♠ K 8
              ♡ Q 10 8 6 4
              ◇ Q 9 2
              ♣ 10 8 2
```

West	North	East	South
Pass	2◇	3♣	4♡ (1)
Pass	Pass	Pass	

(1) Sign-off

The Flannery openers arrived at 4♡ easily. Even if 4♡ had gone down one, minus 50, it would have been worth 7½ matchpoints, as it beats the minus 110 or 130 lost when defending club partials. South bids 4♡ both as a preemptive bid and in the hope of making, since five hearts to the queen and the king doubleton of spades are known to be valuable holdings after a Flannery opening.

20

MYRTLE BEACH REGIONAL, 1984
FINALS OPEN PAIRS

DEALER: South
VULNERABLE: North-South
CONTRACT: 3♡
DECLARER: South
NORTH-SOUTH SCORE: +140
TOP ON BOARD: 25
NORTH-SOUTH MATCHPOINTS: 17½
OPENING LEAD: ◊ A

```
              ♠ K J 6 3
              ♡ Q J 8 7 2
              ◊ 9
              ♣ K 9 8
♠ Q 7 5 4 2            ♠ 9 8
♡ —                   ♡ K 10 6 3
◊ A Q 8 6 5           ◊ K 10 4
♣ Q 7 6               ♣ A 10 5 3
              ♠ A 10
              ♡ A 9 5 4
              ◊ J 7 3 2
              ♣ J 4 2
```

West	North	East	South
—	—	—	Pass
Pass	2◊	Pass	3♡ (1)
Pass	Pass	Pass	

(1) Limit bid showing four or more hearts

South chose to invite game by bidding 3♡ rather than
2 NT because he judged that it was more important for
North to know that he had four hearts than for South to
learn North's minor suit distribution. This is frequently
true when the Flannery opening is made in third position
when he may have a light opening bid.

Flannery describes the major suit holding in one bid, and responder holds the controlling hand. 3♡ is a limit raise. Opener would carry on to game with a maximum 14 to 16 HCP.

21

HUDSON SECTIONAL, 1979
MEN'S PAIRS

DEALER: West
VULNERABLE: None
CONTRACT: 4♡
DECLARER: South
NORTH-SOUTH SCORE: +420
TOP ON BOARD: 9
NORTH-SOUTH MATCHPOINTS: 7
OPENING LEAD: ♡2

```
                    ♠ A K 8 5
                    ♡ K Q 9 6 4
                    ◇ K 10 2
                    ♣ 5
    ♠ 10 7                         ♠ Q J 4 3
    ♡ 10 8 2          N            ♡ J 5
    ◇ Q 9 8 3      W     E         ◇ J 6 5 4
    ♣ A Q J 2         S            ♣ K 9 3
                    ♠ 9 6 2
                    ♡ A 7 3
                    ◇ A 7
                    ♣ 10 8 7 6 4
```

West	North	East	South
Pass	2◇	Pass	2♡ (1)
Pass	3◇ (2)	Pass	4♡
Pass	Pass	Pass	

(1) Sign-off
(2) Maximum with a singleton or void in clubs

The upper limit for a Flannery opening is a hand not quite good enough to reverse, that is, to open 1♡ and rebid 2♠.

North, with his near maximum of 15 HCP and good suits, rebid his longer minor despite responder's sign-off. South now knew that he had no wasted values opposite the known singleton or void in clubs, and was able to bid game confidently.

22

MYRTLE BEACH REGIONAL, 1984
MEN'S PAIRS

DEALER: North
VULNERABLE: Both
CONTRACT: 4♡
DECLARER: North
NORTH-SOUTH SCORE: +620
TOP ON BOARD: 12
NORTH-SOUTH MATCHPOINTS: 9½
OPENING LEAD: ◊3

```
                  ♠ J 8 6 4
                  ♡ A K 9 6 5
                  ◊ J
                  ♣ K Q 9
     ♠ K 7 3                      ♠ 9 5 2
     ♡ 4 3          N             ♡ J 8 7
     ◊ A K Q 9 8 2  W     E       ◊ 7 5 4 3
     ♣ A 3          S             ♣ 7 6 5
                  ♠ A Q 10
                  ♡ Q 10 2
                  ◊ 10 6
                  ♣ J 10 8 4 2
```

West	North	East	South
—	2 ◊	Pass	2 NT (1)
3 ◊	3 ♡ (2)	Pass	4 ♡
Pass	Pass	Pass	

(1) Asking opener for further description
(2) Showing one diamond

With a good fit in both majors, South made a game try by bidding 2 NT. When North showed a singleton in diamonds, he knew there had to be a reasonable play for game.

The North players who opened 1♡ were raised to two

126

by South. West bid 3 ◇ and North called 3 ♡. South, not knowing of the fit in both majors or North's distribution, could only pass, missing the laydown game.

23

LANCASTER REGIONAL, 1983
MEN'S PAIRS

DEALER: North
VULNERABLE: None
CONTRACT: 4 ♡
DECLARER: North
NORTH-SOUTH SCORE: +420
TOP ON BOARD: 12
NORTH-SOUTH MATCHPOINTS: 10
OPENING LEAD: ♣9

```
                    ♠ A K 8 4
                    ♡ J 10 8 6 2
                    ◊ K Q 5
                    ♣ 2
      ♠ 10 7 2              N        ♠ Q J 6 5 3
      ♡ A 3          W            E  ♡ K 9 4
      ◊ 7 4                 S       ◊ 10 8 2
      ♣ A K J 7 5 4                 ♣ 9 8
                    ♠ 9
                    ♡ Q 7 5
                    ◊ A J 9 6 3
                    ♣ Q 10 6 3
```

West	North	East	South
—	2 ◊	Pass	2 NT (1)
3 ♣	3 ♡ (2)	Pass	4 ♡
Pass	Pass	Pass	

(1) Asking opener for further description
(2) Showing a singleton club

In a section of thirteen pairs, only the five pairs playing Flannery reached the good 4 ♡ contract.

After responder bid 2 NT to find out about opener's hand West bid 3 ♣. Opener bid 3 ♡ to show his singleton club. (He would have doubled with three or four clubs, passed with two or bid 3 ◊ with none.) South, knowing his partner's distribution, bid 4♡ with the assurance that it would have a reasonable play.

24

DEALER: West
VULNERABLE: East-West
CONTRACT: 6♠
DECLARER: South
NORTH-SOUTH SCORE: +1010
TOP ON BOARD: 12
NORTH-SOUTH MATCHPOINTS: 10
OPENING LEAD: ♠3

```
                    ♠ A 7 4 2
                    ♡ 9 6 5 4 2
                    ◊ —
                    ♣ A K Q 8
    ♠ 10 5 3            N            ♠ J 8
    ♡ Q 10 8 3      W       E        ♡ K J 7
    ◊ A 9 8             S            ◊ 7 6 5 4
    ♣ 9 7 3                          ♣ J 10 6 5
                    ♠ K Q 9 6
                    ♡ A
                    ◊ K Q J 10 3 2
                    ♣ 4 2
```

West	North	East	South
Pass	2◊	Pass	2 NT (1)
Pass	4♣ (2)	Pass	4 NT
Pass	5♡	Pass	6♠
Pass	Pass	Pass	

(1) Asking opener for further description
(2) Showing four clubs and a diamond void

East-West got two match points out of 12 on this hand when North-South reached 6♠ after a Flannery opening.

In the play, declarer won the opening spade lead, pulled trumps and then played the king of diamonds, ruffing out the ace when West covered.

Some pairs playing Flannery opened the North hand with 1♣ because they thought their major suit holding was too weak for the 2♦ bid. Those pairs reached only 4♠.

Any hand with 11 to 16 HCP, four spades and five hearts is a Flannery opening bid, regardless of the honor strength in the majors. The pattern of the hand is more important than the strength of the major suits.

CLEVELAND REGIONAL, 1979
OPEN PAIRS

DEALER: South
VULNERABLE: North-South
CONTRACT: 4♡
DECLARER: South
NORTH-SOUTH SCORE: +620
TOP ON BOARD: 12
NORTH-SOUTH MATCHPOINTS: 10
OPENING LEAD: ♡5

```
                    ♠ A Q 10 6
                    ♡ A J 9 6 2
                    ◊ 4
                    ♣ Q J 6
      ♠ 9 7 3 2                      ♠ K 5
      ♡ 5 3              N           ♡ 7 4
      ◊ A J 3         W     E        ◊ K Q 8 7
      ♣ A 8 7 4          S           ♣ 10 9 5 3 2
                    ♠ J 8 4
                    ♡ K Q 10 8
                    ◊ 10 9 6 5 2
                    ♣ K
```

West	North	East	South
—	—	—	Pass
Pass	2◊	Pass	2 NT (1)
Pass	3♣ (2)	Pass	4♡
Pass	Pass	Pass	

    (1) Asking opener for further description
    (2) Showing three clubs and a singleton diamond

North-South have only 23 high card points, and the spade king is offside. Yet game makes easily because of North's singleton diamond.

The successful game bidder used Flannery. Once again the 2 NT bid enabled South to diagnose the perfect fit.

LANCASTER REGIONAL, 1983
OPEN PAIRS

DEALER: North
VULNERABLE: North-South
CONTRACT: 3♡
DECLARER: South
NORTH-SOUTH SCORE: −100
TOP ON BOARD: 12
NORTH-SOUTH MATCHPOINTS: 11
OPENING LEAD: ♡3

```
                    ♠ A Q 8 7
                    ♡ K J 8 7 6
                    ◊ Q 8
                    ♣ 3 2
  ♠ J 6                          ♠ 10 4 3 2
  ♡ 3 2             N            ♡ A 9 5 4
  ◊ A 6 3       W       E        ◊ J 10 7
  ♣ A Q 10 9 5 4     S          ♣ J 6
                    ♠ K 9 5
                    ♡ Q 10
                    ◊ K 9 5 4 2
                    ♣ K 8 7
```

West	North	East	South
—	2◊	Pass	2 NT (1)
3♣	Pass (2)	Pass	3♡
Pass	Pass	Pass	

(1) Asking opener for further description
(2) Showing 4-5-2-2 minimum

South's 3♡ bid protected his club king from an immediate attack. With a maximum, opener would bid 3♠ or
3 NT over 3♣.

The majority of the field played either in 3 NT or 4♡,
doubled, down two or more tricks. Minus 100 was worth
nearly all the matchpoints.

PITTSBURGH CLUB GAME, 1983

DEALER: West
VULNERABLE: North-South
CONTRACT: 5 ◇
DECLARER: North
NORTH-SOUTH SCORE: +600
TOP ON BOARD: 8
NORTH-SOUTH MATCHPOINTS: 7½
OPENING LEAD: ♠K

```
                    ♠ 10 6 5 2
                    ♡ K Q 9 7 6
                    ◇ A 10 8
                    ♣ A
     ♠ Q J 7                        ♠ A K 9 4 3
     ♡ J 10 4          N            ♡ A 5 3 2
     ◇ J 7 6       W       E        ◇ 5 3
     ♣ 8 7 6 2         S            ♣ 4 3
                    ♠ 8
                    ♡ 8
                    ◇ K Q 9 4 2
                    ♣ K Q J 10 9 5
```

West	North	East	South
Pass	2 ◇	Pass	2 NT (1)
Pass	3 ◇ (2)	Pass	5 ◇
Pass	Pass	Pass	

(1) Asking opener for further description
(2) Showing three diamonds and a singleton club

Only two pairs reached 5 ◇ after a Flannery opening. Two other pairs playing Flannery thought their spade suit was too weak to open 2 ◇, so they opened 1 ♡. East overcalled 1 ♠ and North-South ended up playing a partial in the minor.

As long as you have the point count, open 2 ◇ regardless of how weak your major suits are. Example:

♠ 10 8 6 4
♡ J 7 6 5 4
◇ A K
♣ A x

Open 2 ◇ . You are giving partner a description of your distribution and your overall high card strength, not the strength in your majors.

28

DEALER: North
VULNERABLE: East-West
CONTRACT: 3 ♡
DECLARER: North
NORTH-SOUTH SCORE: −50
TOP ON BOARD: 12
NORTH-SOUTH MATCHPOINTS: 2
OPENING LEAD: ♡ 4

```
                    ♠ K 9 8 7
                    ♡ K Q 10 8 7
                    ◇ A 5
                    ♣ 3 2
    ♠ 10 2              N            ♠ Q J 6 5 4
    ♡ A 6 5 3       W     E          ♡ 9 4
    ◇ K 7 4 3          S             ◇ Q 8 6
    ♣ A 9 8                          ♣ J 10 4
                    ♠ A 3
                    ♡ J 2
                    ◇ J 10 9 2
                    ♣ K Q 7 6 5
```

West	North	East	South
—	2 ◇	Pass	2 NT (1)
Pass	3 ♡ (2)	Pass	Pass
Pass			

(1) Asking opener for further description
(2) Showing 4-5-2-2 minimum

Listen to the bidding on all hands. Usually it is best to lead a trump against suit contracts when the opponents show signs of a cross ruff. When the opponents open with a Flannery 2 ◇ bid and end up in a suit contract the hand will frequently be played in a cross ruff. Therefore a trump lead is frequently best.

Although the trump lead made the play of the hand more difficult, declarer could have taken nine tricks by playing on diamonds.

29

PITTSBURGH CLUB GAME, 1984

DEALER: West
VULNERABLE: North-South
CONTRACT: 4♡
DECLARER: South
NORTH-SOUTH SCORE: −100
TOP ON BOARD: 12
NORTH-SOUTH MATCHPOINTS: 1
OPENING LEAD: ♡K

```
                    ♠ A K 6 3
                    ♡ Q 10 9 8 4
                    ◇ K 7 4
                    ♣ 7
    ♠ 10 8 5 2              ♠ Q J 4
    ♡ K 2          N         ♡ A 6 3
    ◇ 9 6       W     E      ◇ Q J 8 5
    ♣ K Q 9 4 2    S         ♣ J 6 3
                    ♠ 9 7
                    ♡ J 7 5
                    ◇ A 10 3 2
                    ♣ A 10 8 5
```

West	North	East	South
Pass	2◇	Pass	2 NT (1)
Pass	3◇ (2)	Pass	4♡
Pass	Pass	Pass	

    (1) Asking opener for further description
    (2) Showing three diamonds and a singleton club

After a Flannery opening bid by North, South knew he
had a reasonable play for 4♡ once opener showed a
singleton club. The only way 4♡ can be set is with the
king of hearts lead. When defending against Flannery, it is
generally a good policy to lead a trump.

Those pairs who opened 1♡ with the North hand did
not reach game.

I was defending against this hand and led the king of hearts. Only two other defenders led the king of hearts against 4♡. We were rewarded with eleven matchpoints each on a twelve top.

30

SPRING NATIONALS, 1984
WOMEN'S PAIRS

DEALER: West
VULNERABLE: East-West
CONTRACT: 4♠
DECLARER: South
NORTH-SOUTH SCORE: +450
TOP ON BOARD: 12
NORTH-SOUTH MATCHPOINTS: 8
OPENING LEAD: ♠6

```
              ♠ Q 9 5 2
              ♡ K J 9 5 2
              ◇ A 10
              ♣ K 6
 ♠ 6 4                        ♠ A 8 7
 ♡ Q 7 6 4 3     N            ♡ A 10 8
 ◇ K J 2      W     E         ◇ 8 7 6 4
 ♣ 9 8 7         S            ♣ J 3 2
              ♠ K J 10 3
              ♡ —
              ◇ Q 9 5 3
              ♣ A Q 10 5 4
```

West	North	East	South
Pass	2◇	Pass	2 NT (1)
Pass	3♡ (2)	Pass	4♠
Pass	Pass	Pass	

(1) Asking opener for further description
(2) Showing 4-5-2-2 minimum

Once you find out that North has a semi-balanced minimum, you should give up on slam. A few pairs did bid 6♠, going down one after a spade lead and continuation.

Only if opener responded 3♣ to your 2 NT inquiry would you think about going to 6♠.

140

31

COLUMBUS REGIONAL, 1979
OPEN PAIRS

DEALER: North
VULNERABLE: Both
CONTRACT: 6♡
DECLARER: North
NORTH-SOUTH SCORE: +1430
TOP ON BOARD: 12
NORTH-SOUTH MATCHPOINTS: 11
OPENING LEAD: ♣7

```
                    ♠ A Q J 5
                    ♡ A Q 10 8 3
                    ◊ 9 2
                    ♣ J 6
   ♠ 7                                ♠ 9 4 2
   ♡ 9              ┌─────────┐       ♡ 6 5 2
   ◊ J 5 4 3        │    N    │       ◊ K Q 10 8
   ♣ A K Q 10 8 4 2 │  W   E  │       ♣ 7 5 3
                    │    S    │
                    └─────────┘
                    ♠ K 10 8 6 3
                    ♡ K J 7 4
                    ◊ A 7 6
                    ♣ 9
```

West	North	East	South
—	2◊	Pass	2 NT (1)
4♣	Pass (2)	Pass	4 NT
Pass	5♡	Pass	6♡
Pass	Pass	Pass	

(1) Asking opener for further description
(2) Showing two clubs and a minimum hand (11-14 HCP)

This hand was played by a pair who used Flannery. They bid and made 6♡ and received 11 out of 12 matchpoints. When North opened 1♡ or 1♠, West preempted to 4♣ over whatever South responded. It was difficult for North-South to evaluate their hands, not knowing the fits in two suits and the singleton club, so they stopped at 4♠ or 4♡.

South's decision to bid 6♡ rather than 6♠ is of interest. Knowing that North had 4-5-2-2 distribution, South was aware that he would be able to pitch North's second diamond on his long spades and ruff his two diamond losers if they were playing in a heart contract. If they were playing in spades, one pitch on North's fifth heart would be of no value.

32

COLUMBUS REGIONAL, 1984
OPEN PAIRS

DEALER: West
VULNERABLE: Both
CONTRACT: 3♡
DECLARER: South
NORTH-SOUTH SCORE: +140
TOP ON BOARD: 12
NORTH-SOUTH MATCHPOINTS: 10
OPENING LEAD: ◊9

```
                    ♠ A Q 7 5
                    ♡ K 9 8 5 3
                    ◊ A 7 4
                    ♣ 6
     ♠ J 10 6            N         ♠ K 9 4 2
     ♡ 10 6        W         E     ♡ J 7 2
     ◊ 9 8 6            S         ◊ K Q J 10
     ♣ A J 10 7 3                 ♣ 4 2
                    ♠ 8 3
                    ♡ A Q 4
                    ◊ 5 3 2
                    ♣ K Q 9 8 5
```

West	North	East	South
Pass	2◊	Pass	2 NT (1)
Pass	3◊ (2)	Double	3♡
Pass	Pass	Pass	

(1) Asking opener for further description
(2) Showing three diamonds and a singleton club

Despite 11 HCP, a good five card suit and strong heart fit, South devalued his club honors and worthless diamonds when he learned his partner had a singleton club.

North would continue on to game with extra values (a good 14 to 16 HCP).

33

PITTSBURGH CLUB GAME, 1983

DEALER: North
VULNERABLE: None
CONTRACT: 3♣
DECLARER: West
NORTH-SOUTH SCORE: +50
TOP ON BOARD: 8
NORTH-SOUTH MATCHPOINTS: 7½
OPENING LEAD: ♡K

```
                    ♠ J752
                    ♡ AK982
                    ◊ Q3
                    ♣ K7
        ♠ A93                    ♠ KQ1064
        ♡ 1065        N          ♡ J7
        ◊ A10      W   E         ◊ J742
        ♣ AQ1098      S          ♣ 64
                    ♠ 8
                    ♡ Q43
                    ◊ K9865
                    ♣ J532
```

West	North	East	South
—	2◊	Pass	2♡
3♣	Pass	Pass	Pass

Should you refuse to open Flannery when one or both of your suits are weak? No. Establishing the major suit shape in one bid is very important.

On this hand the Flannery bidders got an unexpected dividend when their opponents were shut out of the spade suit.

After a 1♡ bid by North, most opponents played in spades, making three or four.

SPRING NATIONALS, 1984
OPEN PAIRS

DEALER: South
VULNERABLE: North-South
CONTRACT: 3♡
DECLARER: South
NORTH-SOUTH SCORE: +140
TOP ON BOARD: 12
NORTH-SOUTH MATCHPOINTS: 8½
OPENING LEAD: ◇K

```
                    ♠ A 6 4 3
                    ♡ K Q J 8 6
                    ◇ 4
                    ♣ 9 4 3
    ♠ K J 10 5                      ♠ Q 9 2
    ♡ 5 2           N              ♡ A 10
    ◇ K Q J 10    W   E            ◇ A 8 6 5 2
    ♣ J 10 7        S              ♣ K 8 6
                    ♠ 8 7
                    ♡ 9 7 4 3
                    ◇ 9 7 3
                    ♣ A Q 5 2
```

West	North	East	South
—	—	—	Pass
Pass	2◇	Pass	2♡
Double	Pass	3◇	3♡
Pass	Pass	Pass	

By opening a Flannery 2◇, you take two rounds of bidding away from the opponents and put a lot of pressure on them. Even though the opponents did enter the auction, they could not tell whether 3♡ was a make or if they had a good save at 4◇. It becomes a guessing game and whoever makes the right decision comes out with more matchpoints.

35

FALL CHARITY GAME, 1983

DEALER: South
VULNERABLE: East-West
CONTRACT: 3 ◊ Doubled
DECLARER: East
NORTH-SOUTH SCORE: − 670
TOP ON BOARD: 11
NORTH-SOUTH MATCHPOINTS: 4
OPENING LEAD: ♠2

```
                    ♠ A K 10 9
                    ♡ K 7 4 3 2
                    ◊ 9
                    ♣ 9 7 3
    ♠ Q 8 7 5 4         N          ♠ —
    ♡ J 8 6                        ♡ A Q 9
    ◊ K            W       E       ◊ J 8 7 6 4 3 2
    ♣ K J 5 2         S            ♣ A Q 8
                    ♠ J 6 3 2
                    ♡ 10 5
                    ◊ A Q 10 5
                    ♣ 10 6 4
```

West	North	East	South
—	—	—	Pass
Pass	2 ◊	3 ◊	Double
Pass	Pass	Pass	

I admit it. The Flannery Convention did not help South on this hand. Still other North and South pairs fared as badly or worse, and the inelegant score of −670 still scored four matchpoints out of eleven.

Against 3 ◊ doubled, South elected to lead the two of spades. Persisting in spades every time he was on lead promoted a fourth diamond trick, holding declarer to his contract.

36

PITTSBURGH CLUB GAME, 1980

DEALER: North
VULNERABLE: Both
CONTRACT: 5♣ Doubled
DECLARER: East
NORTH-SOUTH SCORE: +800
TOP ON BOARD: 12
NORTH-SOUTH MATCHPOINTS: 12
OPENING LEAD: ♣3

```
                    ♠ A 10 9 4
                    ♡ A J 5 4 2
                    ◇ Q 4
                    ♣ K 10
      ♠ 7 6 2                       ♠ K J 5
      ♡ K Q 10 9 8 7 3      N       ♡ —
      ◇ —                 W   E     ◇ A J 8 6 5
      ♣ 8 6 4               S       ♣ A Q J 5 2
                    ♠ Q 8 3
                    ♡ 6
                    ◇ K 10 9 7 3 2
                    ♣ 9 7 3
```

West	North	East	South
—	2◇	Double	Pass (1)
3♡	Pass	4◇	Double
4♡	Double	5♣	Double
Pass	Pass	Pass	

(1) Showing diamonds

East should not double the Flannery opening bid. He should bid 2 NT, a takeout for the minors, and West should then bid 3♡, showing long, strong hearts, not 3♣. West has five sure winners at a heart contract.

Since East did double and West jumped to 3♡, West should have passed. This is the only contract that will make at the three level.

DAYTON REGIONAL, 1984
MIXED PAIRS

DEALER: North
VULNERABLE: None
CONTRACT: 3 NT
DECLARER: East
NORTH-SOUTH SCORE: −430
TOP ON BOARD: 12
NORTH-SOUTH MATCHPOINTS: 4½
OPENING LEAD: ♡5

```
                    ♠ A Q 3 2
                    ♡ K Q 10 8 6
                    ◇ 2
                    ♣ 9 6 2
    ♠ J 10 8 7 5         N        ♠ K 9
    ♡ A 4 3         W        E    ♡ J 9 7 2
    ◇ K 10 8            S         ◇ A Q 9 5
    ♣ A 8                         ♣ K Q J
                    ♠ 6 4
                    ♡ 5
                    ◇ J 7 6 4 3
                    ♣ 10 7 5 4 3
```

West	North	East	South
—	2 ◇	2 NT	Pass
3 NT	Pass	Pass	Pass

Flannery kept North-South out of trouble on this hand. Those pairs who opened 1♠ with four spades and five hearts were in for a big penalty — minus 900 or more in 2♠ doubled.

When East doubled the 1♠ opening bid, West passed for penalty and North tried to escape by bidding 2♡, which was doubled by East. South then made a preference bid of 2♠ which was doubled by West.

38

PITTSBURGH CLUB GAME, 1983

DEALER: North
VULNERABLE: Both
CONTRACT: 2◊ Doubled
DECLARER: North
NORTH-SOUTH SCORE: +380
TOP ON BOARD: 8
NORTH-SOUTH MATCHPOINTS: 8
OPENING LEAD: ♣A

```
                    ♠ K 4 3 2
                    ♡ A K 5 4 2
                    ◊ K 10 4
                    ♣ K
     ♠ A J 10 7 5                    ♠ Q 9 6
     ♡ 9 8 7 6 3        N           ♡ 10
     ◊ 3             W     E        ◊ A J 8 2
     ♣ 7 5              S           ♣ A J 10 8 2
                    ♠ 8
                    ♡ Q J
                    ◊ Q 9 7 6 5
                    ♣ Q 9 6 4 3
```

West	North	East	South
—	2◊	Double	Pass (1)
Pass	Pass		

(1) Showing four or more diamonds, short in majors

There was not much to the play. After the lead of the ace of clubs, declarer lost one club, two diamonds and one spade.

Usually at low level contracts it is best to lead a trump. East's best lead against the 2◊ contract was the two of diamonds. When he gets in with the ace of clubs, he can play ace and another diamond. This may hold declarer to two.

East made a bad double. West thought East was long in

149

diamonds and had no reason to bid, knowing opener has four spades and five hearts.

You can see that East-West had a spade partial. 2♠ cannot be beaten.

The field played in a heart partial making two for +110. Note that although East intended his double to show diamonds, it is recommended that the double be used to show a strong, balanced hand, equivalent to a strong 1 NT opening bid.

39

PITTSBURGH SECTIONAL, 1979
MEN'S PAIRS

DEALER: West
VULNERABLE: None
CONTRACT: 4♣ Doubled
DECLARER: East
NORTH-SOUTH SCORE: +300
TOP ON BOARD: 8
NORTH-SOUTH MATCHPOINTS: 7
OPENING LEAD: ♡3

```
                  ♠ A Q 9 8
                  ♡ K Q 10 9 8
                  ◊ 9 7 5 2
                  ♣ —
    ♠ K 10 4                      ♠ 7 5 3
    ♡ 6 5 4 2        N            ♡ A
    ◊ J 6 3        W   E          ◊ K 8 4
    ♣ A 8 7          S            ♣ K Q J 5 4 2
                  ♠ J 6 2
                  ♡ J 7 3
                  ◊ A Q 10
                  ♣ 10 9 6 3
```

West	North	East	South
Pass	2◊	3♣	3♡
4♣	Pass	Pass	Double
Pass	Pass	Pass	

Over North's Flannery opening, East bid 3♣. South bid 3♡, a good competitive call.

West, who was not under pressure, bid 4♣ which was passed around to South, who doubled. This contract was set two tricks.

40

FALL CHARITY GAME, 1983

DEALER: South
VULNERABLE: North-South
CONTRACT: 3♠
DECLARER: South
NORTH-SOUTH SCORE: +140
TOP ON BOARD: 11
NORTH-SOUTH MATCHPOINTS: 9
OPENING LEAD: ♣Q

```
              ♠ A 10 6 2
              ♡ K Q 7 5 2
              ◇ 6 3 2
              ♣ K
  ♠ 3                        ♠ K 8 4
  ♡ J 10 9 8 3      N        ♡ A 6
  ◇ K J 9 5 4   W  °  E      ◇ Q 10
  ♣ Q J            S         ♣ A 9 8 5 4 3
              ♠ Q J 9 7 5
              ♡ 4
              ◇ A 8 7
              ♣ 10 7 6 2
```

West	North	East	South
—	—	—	Pass
Pass	2◇	3♣	3♠
Pass	Pass	Pass	

Competitive auctions are much easier when partner's exact length in the major suits is known.

Here, South might be tempted to bid 4♠. However, since North is in third seat where a Flannery bid may be opened light, South should bid only 3♠. North may continue to game if he has extra values.

After a club lead, the defenders can defeat the contract. Assuming a diamond switch at trick two, declarer must hold up the diamond ace for one round in order to cut the defenders' communications. West overtakes his partner's diamond queen to lead his singleton trump (best defense). No matter how declarer squirms, he must now lose five tricks.

41

SPRING NATIONALS, 1984
SIDE GAME

DEALER: South
VULNERABLE: Neither
CONTRACT: 3 NT
DECLARER: West
NORTH-SOUTH SCORE: −400
TOP ON BOARD: 12
NORTH-SOUTH MATCHPOINTS: 1
OPENING LEAD: ♠ A

```
                    ♠ A K Q 5
                    ♡ Q 7 6 4 3
                    ◊ 8 6 4
                    ♣ 8
  ♠ 8 3 2                        ♠ 10 9 4
  ♡ A J              N           ♡ K 10 8
  ◊ K Q 7 3 2    W       E       ◊ A 5
  ♣ J 10 9           S           ♣ A K 6 3 2
                    ♠ J 7 6
                    ♡ 9 5 2
                    ◊ J 10 9
                    ♣ Q 7 5 4
```

West	North	East	South
—	—	—	Pass
Pass	2 ◊	Pass	2 ♡
3 ◊	Pass	3 ♡	Pass
3 NT	Pass	Pass	Pass

This hand is not a success for the Flannery convention. I was sitting West when North opened 2 ◊, Flannery, against me. When South signed off in 2 ♡, I overcalled 3 ◊. Partner cue bid 3 ♡ and I tried 3 notrump, since I knew the opponents could take at the most four spade tricks.

If we had been vulnerable, I would have passed 2 ♡ and all the pressure would have been on East. I don't think we would have reached 3 NT.

The North players who opened with 1 ♠ kept the East-West pairs out of 3 NT.

42

PITTSBURGH CLUB GAME, 1984

DEALER: North
VULNERABLE: North-South
CONTRACT: 4◇
DECLARER: West
NORTH-SOUTH SCORE: +50
TOP ON BOARD: 8
NORTH-SOUTH MATCHPOINTS: 7
OPENING LEAD: ♡K

```
                    ♠ A J 7 3
                    ♡ A K 10 9 5
                    ◇ K 3
                    ♣ 7 5
    ♠ Q 4                         ♠ K 10 8
    ♡ 8 7              N          ♡ 6 4 3 2
    ◇ A 10 9 7 5 4   W   E        ◇ Q J 8 6
    ♣ K Q 10          S          ♣ A J
                    ♠ 9 6 5 2
                    ♡ Q J
                    ◇ 2
                    ♣ 9 8 6 4 3 2
```

West	North	East	South
—	2◇	Pass	2♠
3◇	Pass	3♠	Pass
4◇	Pass	Pass	Pass

After a Flannery opening and a sign-off bid of 2♡, 2♠, or 3♣, the opponents are under pressure. When one opponent overcalls, his partner has a difficult time evaluating his hand and sometimes gets too high, because it is not known if opener has a minimum or maximum hand, or if responder has any points at all.

When this hand was opened either 1♡ or 1♠, responder passed and West reopened with 2◇ and played the hand at either 2 or 3◇, making three for +110.

43

DEALER: North
VULNERABLE: Both
CONTRACT: 2 NT
DECLARER: West
NORTH-SOUTH SCORE: −150
TOP ON BOARD: 8
NORTH-SOUTH MATCHPOINTS: 6
OPENING LEAD: ♠ 2

```
                    ♠ A 9 8 2
                    ♡ Q 10 9 7 2
                    ◊ 8
                    ♣ A J 3
     ♠ K Q J           N          ♠ 10 6
     ♡ K J 8                       ♡ A 5 4
     ◊ A K 7 6      W     E        ◊ J 10 3
     ♣ Q 8 6           S          ♣ K 9 7 4 2
                    ♠ 7 5 4 3
                    ♡ 6 3
                    ◊ Q 9 5 4 2
                    ♣ 10 5
```

West	North	East	South
—	2 ◊	Pass	2 ♠
2 NT	Pass	Pass	Pass

This hand demonstrates the difficulty in accurately
showing a strong hand, such as West held, after a Flannery
opening bid. East should have raised to 3 NT, but it would
have resulted in the same matchpoint score.

North led the spade two instead of a heart, because
South showed more spades than hearts. The spade lead
held declarer to nine tricks. Most of the field took ten
tricks after a heart lead.

Two other East-West pairs played in a club partial after
a Flannery opening.

44

WEST VIRGINIA CLUB GAME, 1984

DEALER: North
VULNERABLE: Both
CONTRACT: 3 ◊
DECLARER: West
NORTH-SOUTH SCORE: −130
TOP ON BOARD: 12
NORTH-SOUTH MATCHPOINTS: 11
OPENING LEAD: ♠ K

```
                        ♠ A K 5 4
                        ♡ A J 9 8 3
                        ◊ 5 2
                        ♣ Q 2
        ♠ Q 6 2              N            ♠ J 7 3
        ♡ 7 5                             ♡ K Q 10 2
        ◊ A Q J 10 7 3    W     E         ◊ 9 6
        ♣ A 4                S            ♣ K J 6 5
                        ♠ 10 9 8
                        ♡ 6 4
                        ◊ K 8 4
                        ♣ 10 9 8 7 3
```

West	North	East	South
—	2 ◊	Pass	2 ♠
3 ◊	Pass	Pass	Pass

This hand demonstrates the difficulties Flannery creates for opponents, even when they hold the balance of power.

The East-West field bid to 3 NT, making four. Even if diamonds break 4-1, East has other chances with his heart and club holding. This is especially true if the opening lead, unguided by the Flannery opening and responses, is a heart rather than a spade.

Against the Flannery opening, the opponents reached only 3 ◊, since East thought little of his aceless hand containing no spade stopper and only two diamonds.

45

DEALER: North
VULNERABLE: North-South
CONTRACT: 7♠
DECLARER: North
NORTH-SOUTH SCORE: +2210
NORTH-SOUTH IMP SCORE: +13
OPENING LEAD: ♠2

```
                    ♠ K Q J 5
                    ♡ A K 7 6 2
                    ◊ J 9 4
                    ♣ Q
    ♠ —                           ♠ 10 6 4 3 2
    ♡ Q 10 9 5 3         N         ♡ J 8
    ◊ Q 10 6 3 2     W     E       ◊ K 8
    ♣ 7 6 3             S          ♣ J 9 4 2
                    ♠ A 9 8 7
                    ♡ 4
                    ◊ A 7 5
                    ♣ A K 10 8 5
```

West	North	East	South
—	2◊	Pass	3◊ (1)
Pass	3♠ (2)	Pass	4 NT
Pass	5◊	Pass	5 NT
Pass	6♡	Pass	7♠
Pass	Pass	Pass	

(1) Asking for spade controls.
(2) Showing 2 controls. A, K, Q are controls.

This hand illustrates the new 3◊ response to a Flannery 2◊ opening.

Use the 3◊ response only when interested in a slam or a grand slam. This bid enables you to find out how many controls opener has in the major suits.

Against the 7♠ contract, East opened the spade two. Declarer cashed all his side suit winners, then cross-ruffed the rest of the hand to take all the tricks. This was a gain of 13 IMPS. At the other table, only 6♠ was bid.

46

SPRING NATIONAL, 1984
KELLY FIELD PAIRS

DEALER: West
VULNERABLE: None
CONTRACT: 6♣
DECLARER: North
NORTH-SOUTH SCORE: +940
TOP ON BOARD: 12
NORTH-SOUTH MATCHPOINTS: 10½
OPENING LEAD: ◇K

```
                    ♠ K 6 4 3
                    ♡ A K 10 5 4
                    ◇ 9 5
                    ♣ A 8
   ♠ Q 9 8                         ♠ A J 10 7 5 2
   ♡ J 9 8 3          N            ♡ 7 6
   ◇ J 10 6 4     W       E        ◇ K Q 3 2
   ♣ 5 4              S            ♣ 7
                    ♠ —
                    ♡ Q 2
                    ◇ A 8 7
                    ♣ K Q J 10 9 6 3 2
```

West	North	East	South
Pass	2◇	2♠	3◇ (1)
Pass	3♡ (2)	Pass	3♠ (3)
Pass	4♣ (4)	Pass	4 NT
Pass	5♡	Pass	6♣
Pass	Pass	Pass	

(1) Asking for spade controls.
(2) Showing one spade control.
(3) Asking for heart controls.
(4) Showing two heart controls.

The 3 ◇ response over a Flannery 2 ◇ opening now has
a new meaning. This bid now asks for controls in the

major suits when interested in a slam. If opener had shown no spade controls, responder could have found out exactly which honors partner held in the heart suit. On the actual hand, by bidding Blackwood he finds that opener has the ace of hearts and either the ace of spades or the king of spades and the ace of clubs. The grand slam could have been bid if opener had shown three aces.

I checked this hand across the field and found that six or fewer of thirteen pairs in each section bid 6♣.

47

WEST VIRGINIA, 1983
CLUB GAME

DEALER: South
VULNERABLE: None
CONTRACT: 4♠
DECLARER: North
NORTH-SOUTH SCORE: +480
TOP ON BOARD: 12
NORTH-SOUTH MATCHPOINTS: 11
OPENING LEAD: ◊ A

```
                    ♠ Q 10 9 5
                    ♡ A Q 10 5 2
                    ◊ 10
                    ♣ Q 8 4
   ♠ J 7                          ♠ 8 3
   ♡ J 7 4            N           ♡ 9 8
   ◊ K Q 8 7 3    W     E         ◊ A J 6 4
   ♣ A 9 5            S           ♣ K J 10 6 2
                    ♠ A K 6 4 2
                    ♡ K 6 3
                    ◊ 9 5 2
                    ♣ 7 3
```

West	North	East	South
—	—	—	Pass
Pass	2 ◊	Pass	4 ◊ (1)
Double	4 ♠	Pass	Pass
Pass			

(1) Transfer to 4 ♠

After a Flannery opening bid by North, South, with no
tenaces in the minors, made a transfer bid of 4 ◊, asking
North to bid 4♠. East led the ace of diamonds and
continued with the diamond four. Since North's hand was
concealed, East did not know that a shift to clubs was
needed at trick two to hold declarer to ten tricks.

At the tables where North opened 1 ♡ South became the declarer in 4 ♠. With the North hand exposed, it was easy for West, after leading the king of diamonds, to shift to ace and another club, holding declarer to ten tricks.

PITTSBURGH CLUB GAME, 1984

DEALER: North
VULNERABLE: East-West
CONTRACT: 4 ♡
DECLARER: North
NORTH-SOUTH SCORE: +420
TOP ON BOARD: 12
NORTH-SOUTH MATCHPOINTS: 9
OPENING LEAD: ♣3

```
                    ♠ Q J 9 2
                    ♡ Q J 10 7 3
                    ◇ K Q 2
                    ♣ K
    ♠ A 10 8 5            N            ♠ 7 4 3
    ♡ 9 6                              ♡ 8 4 2
    ◇ 8 5 3         W         E        ◇ A 9 6
    ♣ A Q 10 4            S            ♣ 9 8 6 3
                    ♠ K 6
                    ♡ A K 5
                    ◇ J 10 7 4
                    ♣ J 7 5 2
```

West	North	East	South
—	2 ◇	Pass	4 ♣ (1)
Double	4 ♡	Pass	Pass
Pass			

(1) Transfer to 4 ♡

Flannery bidders played this hand in 4 ♡, making.

At the tables where North opened the bidding, 1 ♡, 4 ♡ should have been reached, but many pairs landed in 3 NT, down one, after a club lead by West.

PITTSBURGH CLUB GAME, 1983

DEALER: North
VULNERABLE: East-West
CONTRACT: 4♠
DECLARER: North
NORTH-SOUTH SCORE: +450
TOP ON BOARD: 8
NORTH-SOUTH MATCHPOINTS: 7
OPENING LEAD: ◊ J

```
              ♠ A 10 7 4
              ♡ K 10 5 4 2
              ◊ A 7 6
              ♣ A
  ♠ J 8 3            N        ♠ 5 2
  ♡ 7 3         W        E    ♡ A Q 6
  ◊ K Q 8 5 2        S        ◊ J 10 9 4 3
  ♣ Q 8 6                     ♣ K 10 2
              ♠ K Q 9 6
              ♡ J 9 8
              ◊ —
              ♣ J 9 7 5 4 3
```

West	North	East	South
West	*North*	*East*	*South*
—	2 ◊	Pass	4 ◊ (1)
Double	4 ♠	Pass	Pass
Pass			

(1) Transfer to 4 ♠

Since South had no tenaces, he wanted North to be declarer. Therefore, he bid 4 ◊ , a transfer to spades. (4♣ is a transfer to hearts.)

Played from the South hand, a heart lead holds declarer to ten tricks. But after a diamond lead and a slip in the defense, declarer took 11 tricks.

50

DEALER: West
VULNERABLE: East-West
CONTRACT: 4♡
DECLARER: North
NORTH-SOUTH SCORE: +420
TOP ON BOARD: 12
NORTH-SOUTH MATCHPOINTS: 10
OPENING LEAD: ♡10

```
                    ♠ K Q J 8
                    ♡ Q J 9 7 6
                    ◇ K 8 3
                    ♣ 2
     ♠ 9 6 5 2        N          ♠ 7 3
     ♡ 8 4 3      W       E      ♡ 10 5
     ◇ 6 5 2         S          ◇ A Q J 9 4
     ♣ A 10 5                    ♣ J 8 7 4
                    ♠ A 10 4
                    ♡ A K 2
                    ◇ 10 7
                    ♣ K Q 9 6 3
```

West	North	East	South
Pass	2◇	Pass	2 NT (1)
Pass	3◇ (2)	Double	4♣ (3)
Pass	4♡	Pass	Pass
Pass			

(1) Asking opener for further description
(2) Showing three diamonds and a singleton club
(3) Transfer to 4♡

This hand illustrates transfer bids after an opponent
doubles opener's 3♣ or 3◇ response to 2 NT.

4♣ does not ask if partner has a minimum or maximum
hand, as it would with no interference. 4♣ is now a

transfer to 4 ♡ and 4 ◇ a transfer to 4 ♠, as it is frequently necessary to protect opener's minor suit cards after a lead-directing double.

The double of 3 ◇ also helped South determine not to try for slam, holding two small diamonds.

51

WORLD CHAMPIONSHIP, 1979

DEALER: North
VULNERABLE: North-South
TABLE 1
  CONTRACT: 3 ◇
  DECLARER: West - Italy
  NORTH-SOUTH SCORE: +50
TABLE 2
  CONTRACT: 2 ◇
  DECLARER: West - USA
  NORTH-SOUTH SCORE: −90
RESULTS: USA +4 IMPS

```
                    ♠ A 6 3 2
                    ♡ A K 7 6 4
                    ◇ 8 6 4
                    ♣ 7
     ♠ 10 5              N          ♠ K Q J 8
     ♡ 10 8 5 3      W       E      ♡ Q
     ◇ A 7 5 3          S          ◇ Q J 9
     ♣ 6 4 3                        ♣ A Q J 9 5
                    ♠ 9 7 4
                    ♡ J 9 2
                    ◇ K 10 2
                    ♣ K 10 8 2
```

TABLE 1

West	North	East	South
—	2 ◇	2 ♠ (1)	Pass
3 ◇	Pass	Pass	Pass

         (1) Takeout double with spades

TABLE 2

West	North	East	South
—	1 ♡	Double	Pass
2 ◇	Pass	Pass	Pass

At Table 1, when Italy came into the auction after USA opened Flannery, they were headed for a minus score because they were forced to compete at a higher level than at the other table.

This hand demonstrates some of the preemptive value of the Flannery opening.

52

WORLD CHAMPIONSHIP, 1979

DEALER: North
VULNERABLE: East-West
TABLE 1
  CONTRACT: 3 NT
  DECLARER: South - USA
  NORTH-SOUTH SCORE: +460
TABLE 2
  CONTRACT: 6 NT
  DECLARER: South - Far East
  NORTH-SOUTH SCORE: −50
RESULT: USA +11 IMPS

```
                    ♠ K J 7 4
                    ♡ A Q J 10 7
                    ◇ 7
                    ♣ Q 10 4
    ♠ A 9 6 5 3 2       N        ♠ 10
    ♡ 5 3          W        E    ♡ K 8 4
    ◇ 9 5 3                      ◇ Q J 8 6 4 2
    ♣ 7 6               S        ♣ 9 8 5
                    ♠ Q 8
                    ♡ 9 6 2
                    ◇ A K 10
                    ♣ A K J 3 2
```

TABLE 1

West	North	East	South
—	2 ◇	Pass	2 NT (1)
Pass	3 ♣ (2)	Pass	3 NT
Pass	Pass	Pass	

    (1) Asking opener for further description
    (2) Showing three clubs and a singleton diamond

The USA pair was content to play 3 NT, with South's poor major suit holding. Even with North's strong majors and the club queen, 6 NT requires a heart finesse.

53

BUFFALO REGIONAL, 1983
SWISS TEAMS

DEALER: North
VULNERABLE: Both
CONTRACT: 6♡
DECLARER: North
NORTH-SOUTH SCORE: +1430
NORTH-SOUTH IMPS: +13
OPENING LEAD: ♣5

```
              ♠ K J 6 5
              ♡ A J 8 5 2
              ◊ —
              ♣ A 10 8 2
  ♠ 8 7 2                      ♠ Q 9 4
  ♡ 7              N           ♡ K 3
  ◊ K Q 9 5 2    W   E         ◊ J 10 8 4 3
  ♣ J 9 6 4        S           ♣ Q 7 5
              ♠ A 10 3
              ♡ Q 10 9 6 4
              ◊ A 7 6
              ♣ K 3
```

West	North	East	South
—	2◊	Pass	2 NT (1)
Pass	4♣ (2)	Pass	4 NT
Pass	5♡	Pass	6♡

(1) Asking opener for further description
(2) Showing four clubs and a void in diamonds

With strong controls and five card support, South pressed on to a slam after a Flannery opening, despite his wasted diamond ace.

Declarer stripped the hands of the minor suits, cashing the ace of hearts in the process. He then exited with a heart to endplay whichever opponent won the trick.

54

MYRTLE BEACH REGIONAL, 1984
MASTER'S TEAMS

DEALER: West
VULNERABLE: North-South
CONTRACT: 6 ♡
DECLARER: South
NORTH-SOUTH SCORE: +1430
NORTH-SOUTH IMPS: +13
OPENING LEAD: ◊ 4

```
                    ♠ K Q 8 5
                    ♡ K Q 9 4 3
                    ◊ 8
                    ♣ K 8 3
     ♠ 6 4             N            ♠ J 10 7 3
     ♡ J 6 5       W       E        ♡ 7
     ◊ 4 2             S            ◊ K Q 10 9 3
     ♣ Q J 9 7 5 2                  ♣ A 10 4
                    ♠ A 9 2
                    ♡ A 10 8 2
                    ◊ A J 7 6 5
                    ♣ 6
```

West	North	East	South
Pass	2 ◊	Double	2 NT (1)
Pass	3 ♣ (2)	Pass	6 ♡
Pass	Pass	Pass	

(1) Asking opener for further description
(2) Showing three clubs and a singleton diamond

With the known fit in two suits plus top controls, South proceeded to slam after opener showed a singleton diamond. He knew he would have a reasonable play for slam, if not a laydown. Even with the ace of clubs wrong, and spades breaking 4-2, South made the slam. After losing to the ace of clubs, he ruffed two clubs and two diamonds to arrive at the following position:

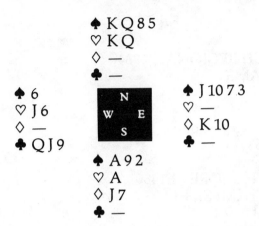

```
            ♠ K Q 8 5
            ♡ K Q
            ◇ —
            ♣ —
  ♠ 6              ♠ J 10 7 3
  ♡ J 6       N    ♡ —
  ◇ —     W       E  ◇ K 10
  ♣ Q J 9      S   ♣ —
            ♠ A 9 2
            ♡ A
            ◇ J 7
            ♣ —
```

South cashed the ace of hearts and led a spade to the king. When he now cashed the king of hearts, East was squeezed in diamonds and spades. If the spades were 3-3, declarer would have had no problem, but if spades were 4-2, he played so that if the hand with four spades also had the king of diamonds he could not protect both suits when the last heart was played.

At the other table, North-South bid only to 4 ♡, making six.

55

**NORTH CAROLINA REGIONAL
SWISS TEAMS**

DEALER: North
VULNERABLE: Both
TABLE 1
  CONTRACT: 6♠
  DECLARER: South
  NORTH-SOUTH SCORE: +1430
TABLE 2
  CONTRACT: 4♠
  DECLARER: South
  NORTH-SOUTH SCORE: +680
NORTH-SOUTH TABLE 1 RESULT: +13 IMPS
OPENING LEAD: ◇K

```
                    ♠ Q 10 6 2
                    ♡ K Q J 7 3
                    ◇ 4
                    ♣ A 10 3
    ♠ 5                         ♠ J 8 3
    ♡ A 4              N        ♡ 10 9 6 5
    ◇ K Q J 9 7 6 2  W   E     ◇ 5 3
    ♣ J 9 5              S      ♣ Q 8 7 2
                    ♠ A K 9 7 4
                    ♡ 8 2
                    ◇ A 10 8
                    ♣ K 6 4
```

TABLE 1

West	North	East	South
—	2◇	Pass	2 NT (1)
3◇	3♡ (2)	Pass	4 NT
Pass	5◇	Pass	6♠

  (1) Asking opener for further description
  (2) Showing one diamond

Playing in a Swiss Team event, our partners bid and made 6♠ while our opponents stopped at 4♠ after West preempted to 4◇ over a 1♠ response by South.

We won 13 IMPS on this hand. It was easy for our partners to bid 6♠. South knew the exact distribution of North's hand after the second round of the auction. Flannery removed a lot of the guesswork from the hand. Should North bid 4♠ over West's 4◇ bid? If North passes, South doubles and North bids 4♠, should South make a slam try? If South does make a slam try, should North accept because of his four spades, source of tricks in hearts and controls in both minors, or should he reject because of his lack of aces and generally minimum hand? Flannery resolves these problems by defining both distribution and high card strength immediately. North would then be able to freely cooperate with any slam tries having already defined his hand.

56

SPINGOLD, 1983

DEALER: South
VULNERABLE: North-South
TABLE 1
   CONTRACT: 4 ◊
   DECLARER: East
   NORTH-SOUTH SCORE: +100
TABLE 2
   CONTRACT: 4 ♡
   DECLARER: North
   NORTH-SOUTH SCORE: +620
NORTH-SOUTH TABLE 2 RESULT: +11 IMPS

TABLE 3
   CONTRACT: 4 ♡
   DECLARER: North
   NORTH-SOUTH SCORE: +620
TABLE 4
   CONTRACT: 4 ♡
   DECLARER: South
   NORTH-SOUTH SCORE: −100
NORTH-SOUTH TABLE 3 RESULT: +12 IMPS

```
                    ♠ Q 10 9 5
                    ♡ A J 6 4
                    ◊ Q
                    ♣ Q 10 8 7
       ♠ J 7 4                    ♠ 6 2
       ♡ 7 2            N         ♡ Q 5
       ◊ J 10 5 3    W     E      ◊ A K 9 8 7 2
       ♣ K 9 4 3        S         ♣ A 5 2
                    ♠ A K 8 3
                    ♡ K 10 9 8 3
                    ◊ 6 4
                    ♣ J 6
```

TABLE 1

South	West	North	East
Pass	Pass	Pass	1 ◊
1 ♡	2 ◊	3 ◊	4 ◊

4 ◊ down two
North-South: +100

TABLE 2

South	West	North	East
2 ◊	Pass	4 ♡	Pass
Pass	Pass		

4 ♡ making four
North-South: +620

TABLE 3

South	West	North	East
2 ◊	Pass	4 ♡	Pass
Pass	Pass		

4 ♡ making four
North-South: +620

TABLE 4

South	West	North	East
1 ♡	Pass	3 ♡	4 ◊
4 ♡	Pass	Pass	Pass

4 ♡ down one
North-South: −100

The Flannery bidders at Tables 2 and 3 reached 4 ♡ easily since North knew about the double fit in the majors. After ruffing the second diamond lead, declarer cashed the top hearts to score game. This is the best play missing four trumps with no adverse bidding.

At Table 4, South's decision to bid 4 ♡ with 4-5-2-2 distribution was a guess, since neither North or South knew about the hidden spade fit. South was unfortunate to lose the setting trick to the heart queen when he played East for shortness in hearts based on his 4 ◊ call.

Not knowing about the double fit undoubtedly contributed to the poor results at Table 1. With 2½ quick tricks and his high cards in the majors, South has a clear Flannery opener. As it was he chose to pass the hand and East-West bought the contract for 4 ◊ , down two for an 11 IMP loss to North-South.

57

BUFFALO REGIONAL, 1983
MASTER'S TEAMS

DEALER: West
VULNERABLE: None
CONTRACT: 6 ♠
DECLARER: South
NORTH-SOUTH SCORE: +980
NORTH-SOUTH IMP RESULT: +11 IMPS
OPENING LEAD: ◊ K

```
                    ♠ Q J 10 6
                    ♡ K Q J 7 3
                    ◊ 9
                    ♣ Q J 8
        ♠ 8                         ♠ 7 2
        ♡ 9 8 5          N          ♡ A 10 6 4 2
        ◊ A K 8 7 3   W     E       ◊ Q J 6 4
        ♣ 10 6 3 2       S          ♣ 9 4
                    ♠ A K 9 5 4 3
                    ♡ —
                    ◊ 10 5 2
                    ♣ A K 7 5
```

West	North	East	South
Pass	2 ◊	Pass	2 NT (1)
Pass	3 ♣ (2)	Pass	6 ♠
Pass	Pass	Pass	

(1) Asking opener for further description
(2) Showing three clubs and a singleton diamond

Generally, a Flannery opening should contain a minimum of two quick tricks, but North chose to open this hand because of the internal solidity of his major suits. South easily reached slam when North showed a singleton diamond.

At the other table the North-South pair reached only 4 ♠ after a 1 ♡ opening. As the North hand was opened at both tables, the difference between the two final contracts can be attributed to the increased accuracy of the Flannery opening bid over the 1 ♡ opening.

58

WORLD CHAMPIONSHIP, 1979

DEALER: West
VULNERABLE: Both
TABLE 1
   CONTRACT: 4♡
   DECLARER: South
   NORTH-SOUTH SCORE: USA +620
TABLE 2
   CONTRACT: 3 NT
   DECLARER: South
   NORTH-SOUTH SCORE: Italy −100
RESULT: USA +12 IMPS

```
                    ♠ J 10 8 4
                    ♡ A K Q 6 4
                    ◊ Q 5
                    ♣ K 5
    ♠ Q 9 2            N            ♠ K 7 3
    ♡ 9 7         W         E       ♡ J 10 8
    ◊ 9 8 3            S            ◊ K 7 6 4
    ♣ Q 8 7 4 2                     ♣ A J 3
                    ♠ A 6 5
                    ♡ 5 3 2
                    ◊ A J 10 2
                    ♣ 10 9 6
```

TABLE 1

West	North	East	South
Pass	2◊	Pass	3♡ (1)
Pass	4♡	Pass	Pass
Pass			

(1) Limit bid with four or more hearts

West led the nine of hearts. Declarer pulled trump, finessed diamonds and pitched a club on the third diamond. He then led a small spade toward J1084, losing to the king; trumped the club return; led a spade to the

182

ace; and a spade to dummy. Declarer played the hand well, guarding against four spades on his left.

Although the play is more difficult with a club lead, the contract is unbeatable. After the defenders cash two club tricks, declarer wins the third trick in dummy and leads the jack of spades. Presuming that East ducks (best), he will later be squeezed between his K 7 of spades and his king fourth of diamonds.

3♡ was the wrong bid with the South hand. A bid of 3♡ over a Flannery opening shows four card trump support and a good 9 + to 11 HCP, with honor strength in both minors. The proper bid is 2♡. The hand is too balanced to make a game try. If responder held one less spade, and one more club, the proper bid would be 2 NT.

At Table 2, Italy played 3 NT by South, down one when West led a club. USA took the first five tricks.

59

PITTSBURGH CLUB GAME, 1984

DEALER: North
VULNERABLE: None
TABLE 1
   CONTRACT: 5♡
   DECLARER: South
   NORTH-SOUTH SCORE: +450
TABLE 2
   CONTRACT: 5♢ Doubled
   DECLARER: East
   NORTH-SOUTH SCORE: −550
NORTH-SOUTH TABLE 1 RESULT: +14 IMPS

```
                    ♠ A 7 5 4
                    ♡ J 10 9 7 3
                    ♢ 4
                    ♣ A Q 6
        ♠ K J 10 3          ♠ 8 6
        ♡ —           N     ♡ Q 6 5 2
        ♢ A Q 8 7 3  W E    ♢ K J 10 6 5 2
        ♣ 9 8 5 2     S     ♣ 3
                    ♠ Q 9 2
                    ♡ A K 8 4
                    ♢ 9
                    ♣ K J 10 7 4
```

TABLE 1

West	North	East	South
—	2♢	3♢	4♡
5♢	Pass (1)	Pass	5♡
Pass	Pass	Pass	
		(1) Shows 1 Diamond	

184

TABLE 2

West	North	East	South
—	1♡	3◇	4♡
5◇	Double	Pass	Pass
Pass			

At Table 1, 5♡ was bid and made after North's Flannery opening. Opener's pass of the opponent's 5◇ bid showed a singleton diamond, after which South bid 5♡ with confidence, knowing there was a fit in three suits.

At Table 2, North opened 1♡ and the auction was swift. North had to make a decision at the five level. Not knowing of the fit with his partner in three suits, he chose to double 5◇, which made for a doubled game swing.

60

DAYTON REGIONAL, 1984
SWISS TEAMS

DEALER: South
VULNERABLE: None
TABLE 1
  CONTRACT: 6♡
  DECLARER: North
  NORTH-SOUTH SCORE: +980
TABLE 2
CONTRACT: 5♡
  DECLARER: South
  NORTH-SOUTH SCORE: +480
NORTH-SOUTH TABLE 1 RESULT: +11 IMPS

```
              ♠ 7
              ♡ A J 6 2
              ◊ A K 7 3
              ♣ A 10 9 6
♠ A K 6 5 4                    ♠ Q 9 3
♡ 7 3          N               ♡ 5 4
◊ 10 6 4    W     E            ◊ 9 8 5 2
♣ J 7 5        S               ♣ 8 4 3 2
              ♠ J 10 8 2
              ♡ K Q 10 9 8
              ◊ Q J
              ♣ K Q
```

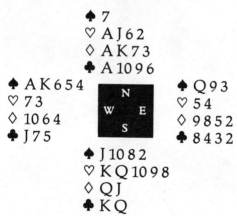

TABLE 1

West	North	East	South
—	—	—	2 ◇
Pass	2 NT (1)	Pass	3 NT (2)
Pass	4 NT	Pass	5 ♣
Pass	6 ♡	Pass	Pass
Pass			

(1) Asking opener for further description
(2) Maximum 4-5-2-2 with Qx or better in both minors; a good 14 or more HCP.

At Table 1, North-South used Flannery to gain 11 IMPS. Over South's rebid of 3 NT North bid the heart slam knowing that his partner had the fillers in the minors.

At Table 2, Flannery was not used and North was unable to find out the exact distribution of the South hand. He stopped in 5 ♡ when South showed no aces after his Blackwood bid.

Today the hand would be bid with more confidence by using the new 3 ◇ bid. The auction would go:

North	South
—	2 ◇
3 ◇ (1)	4 ♣ (2)
4 ◇ (3)	4 ♠ (4)
6 ♡	

(1) Asking for the number of spade controls.
(2) No spade controls.
(3) Asking for the number of heart controls.
(4) Two heart controls.

61

WORLD CHAMPIONSHIPS, 1979

DEALER: North
VULNERABLE: None
TABLE 1
  CONTRACT: 5 ◇ Doubled
  DECLARER: West
  NORTH-SOUTH SCORE: USA +300
TABLE 2
  CONTRACT: 4 ♠
  DECLARER: North
  NORTH-SOUTH SCORE: Italy +420
RESULT: USA −3 IMPS

```
                    ♠ A K Q 6
                    ♡ A J 10 9 6
                    ◇ 8 7
                    ♣ J 10
    ♠ 9 7 5                        ♠ 4 2
    ♡ K 5             N            ♡ 8 7 4 2
    ◇ K J 6 5      W     E         ◇ A Q 10 4 2
    ♣ A 7 6 4         S            ♣ 5 2
                    ♠ J 10 8 3
                    ♡ Q 3
                    ◇ 9 3
                    ♣ K Q 9 8 3
```

TABLE 1

West	North	East	South
—	2 ◇	Double	3 ♠ (1)
4 ♣	4 ♠	Pass	Pass
5 ◇	Double	Pass	Pass
Pass			

(1) Limit bid with at least four spades

If South had been playing the structure recommended in this book he would have bid 2 NT over East's double, not

3 ♠ . 3 ♠ shows values in both minors.

USA lost three IMPS on this deal when they should have won two IMPS. They failed to beat 5 ◊ three tricks when North cashed the ace of hearts. North could have waited, since any heart tricks he had coming were very unlikely to run away.

Note that although East intended his double to show diamonds, it is recommended that the double be used to show a strong balanced hand, equivalent to a 1 NT opening bid. Diamonds can be shown by bidding 3 ◊ . A pass is recommended with East's hand.

62

DAYTON REGIONAL, 1984
SWISS TEAMS

DEALER: West
VULNERABLE: Both
CONTRACT: 6♣
DECLARER: North
NORTH-SOUTH SCORE: +1370
NORTH-SOUTH IMPS: +13
OPENING LEAD: ♦Q

```
                    ♠ A Q 7 4
                    ♡ K Q 9 8 5
                    ♦ 6
                    ♣ J 7 4
    ♠ 10 6 5 2           N          ♠ K J 9 3
    ♡ J 10 4 3       W       E      ♡ 6 2
    ♦ A K 5 4            S          ♦ Q J 10 7 2
    ♣ 8                             ♣ Q 3
                    ♠ 8
                    ♡ A 7
                    ♦ 9 8 3
                    ♣ A K 10 9 6 5 2
```

West	North	East	South
Pass	2♦	Pass	2 NT (1)
Pass	3♣ (2)	Pass	4 NT
Pass	5♦	Pass	6♣
Pass	Pass	Pass	

(1) Asking opener for further description
(2) Showing three clubs and a singleton diamond

Once South learned that North had a singleton diamond, he checked for aces and confidently bid a club slam, with only 23 HCP between the two hands. Almost any hand North held with one ace would make the slam virtually a laydown.

At the other table North-South struggled to get to 5♣ after North opened the bidding with 1♠.

THE BEST OF DEVYN PRESS
Newly Published Bridge Books

WINNING BRIDGE INTANGIBLES
by Mike Lawrence and Keith Hanson \$2.95

This book shows you how to achieve the best results possible with the knowledge you already possess. A few of the topics covered are: how to be a good partner, how to avoid giving the opponents crucial information, how to develop the best attitude at the table, and the best way to form a partnership. Recommended for: beginner through advanced.

THE FLANNERY TWO-DIAMOND CONVENTION
by Bill Flannery \$7.95

Finally, a complete book on the Flannery convention, written by its creator. This teaches you the secrets to success so you will never have a misunderstanding with your partner. Included are sections on the mechanics, defenses against Flannery, the correct opening lead against the opponents' auctions, 62 example hands with explanations, and much more. Recommended for: intermediate through expert.

BRIDGE: THE BIDDER'S GAME
by Dr. George Rosenkranz \$12.95

Bidding for the 80's; the concepts top experts are using today to increase their slam, game, part score, and competitive accuracy. Included are: an introduction to relays and how they can be incorporated into your present system, trump-asking and control-asking bids, new methods of cue bidding, revisions of popular conventions such as Stayman and Splinter bids, a complete update of the Romex System, with hundreds of examples. Recommended for: advanced through expert.

HAVE I GOT A STORY FOR YOU
by Patty Eber and Mike Freeman \$7.95

These are humorous stories on bridge, submitted by players across the country, from the local to national level. Hundreds contributed their favorite tales; these are the best from club games, tournaments, bars and hospitality rooms. This entertaining collection is a perfect gift and is recommended for: anyone who enjoys bridge.

THE ART OF LOGICAL BIDDING
by Andrew Gorski \$4.95

If you're tired of memorizing bidding sequences and still getting mediocre results at the table, this book is for you. It presents a new system, based on the inherent logic of the game. Because of the natural approach it reduces the chances of partnership misunderstandings, so you'll feel confident of reaching the best contract. Recommended for: bright beginner through intermediate.

STANDARD PLAYS OF CARD COMBINATIONS FOR
CONTRACT BRIDGE by Alan Truscott,
Laura Jane Gordy, and Edward L. Gordy \$5.95

Contains the 150 most important card combinations so that you can maximize your trick-taking potential. The one skill that all experts possess is the ability to handle the standard plays correctly; here is this crucial information at your fingertips. Included are plays to the opening lead, suit-handling and finesses, second hand play and third hand play. Perforated so you may remove the cards from the book if you wish. Recommended for: beginner through advanced.

THE BEST OF DEVYN PRESS

Bridge Conventions Complete
by Amalya Kearse
$17.95

An undated and expanded edition (over 800 pages) of the reference book no duplicate player can afford to be without. The reviews say it all:

"At last! A book with both use and appeal for expert or novice plus everybody in between. Every partnership will find material they will wish to add to their present system. Not only are all the conventions in use anywhere today clearly and aptly described, but Kearse criticizes various treatments regarding potential flaws and how they can be circumvented.

"Do yourself a favor and add this book to your shelf even if you don't enjoy most bridge books. This book is a treat as well as a classic."
—ACBL BULLETIN

"A must for duplicate fans, this is a comprehensive, well-written guide through the maze of systems and conventions. This should be particularly useful to those who don't want to be taken off guard by an unfamiliar convention, because previously it would have been necessary to amass several references to obtain all the information presented."
—BRIDGE WORLD MAGAZINE

Published January, 1984

Recommended for: all duplicate players

ISBN 0-910791-07-4 paperback

Test Your Play As Declarer, Volume 1
by Jeff Rubens and Paul Lukacs
$5.95

Any reader who studies this book carefully will certainly become much more adept at playing out a hand. There are 89 hands here, each emphasizing a particular point in declarer play. The solution to each problem explains how and why a declarer should handle his hands in a certain way. A reprint of the original.

Published December, 1983

Recommended for: intermediate through expert

ISBN 0-910791-12-0 paperback

Devyn Press Book of Partnership Understandings
by Mike Lawrence
$2.95

Stop bidding misunderstandings before they occur with this valuable guide. It covers all the significant points you should discuss with your partner, whether you are forming a new partnership or you have played together for years.

Published December, 1983

Recommended for: novice through expert

ISBN 0-910791-08-2 paperback

101 Bridge Maxims
by H. W. Kelsey
$7.95

The experience of a master player and writer condensed into 101 easy-to-understand adages. Each hand will help you remember these essential rules during the heat of battle.

Published December, 1983

Recommended for: bright beginner through advanced.

ISBN 0-910791-10-4 paperback

Play Bridge with Mike Lawrence
by Mike Lawrence
$9.95

Follow Mike through a 2-session matchpoint event at a regional tournament, and learn how to gather information from the auction, the play of the cards and the atmosphere at the table. When to go against the field, compete, make close doubles, and more.

Published December, 1983

Recommended for: bright beginner through expert.

ISBN 0-910791-09-0 paperback

Play These Hands With Me
by Terence Reese
$7.95

Studies 60 hands in minute detail. How to analyze your position and sum up information you have available, with a post-mortem reviewing main points.

Published December, 1983

Recommended for: intermediate through expert.

ISBN 0-910791-11-2 paperback

THE BEST OF DEVYN PRESS
Bridge Books

collection of the world's premier bridge authors have produced, for your
ment, this wide and impressive selection of books.

MATCHPOINTS
by Kit Woolsey
$9.95

The long-awaited second book by the author of the classic *Partnership Defense*. *Matchpoints* examines all of the crucial aspects of duplicate bridge. It is surprising, with the wealth of excellent books on bidding and play, how neglected matchpoint strategy has been—Kit has filled that gap forever with the best book ever written on the subject. The chapters include: general concepts, constructive bidding, competitive bidding, defensive bidding and the play.
Published October, 1982
Recommended for: intermediate through expert.
ISBN 0-910791-00-7 paperback

DYNAMIC DEFENSE
by Mike Lawrence
$9.95

One of the top authors of the '80's has produced a superior work in his latest effort. These unique hands offer you an over-the-shoulder look at how a World Champion reasons through the most difficult part of bridge. You will improve your technique as you sit at the table and attempt to find the winning sequence of plays. Each of the 65 problems is thoroughly explained and analyzed in the peerless Lawrence style.
Published October, 1982.
Recommended for: bright beginner through expert.
ISBN 0-910791-01-5 paperback

MODERN IDEAS IN BIDDING
by Dr. George Rosenkranz and Alan Truscott
$9.95

Mexico's top player combines with the bridge editor of the <u>New York Times</u> to produce a winner's guide to bidding theory. Constructive bidding, slams, pre-emptive bidding, competitive problems, overcalls and many other valuable concepts are covered in depth. Increase your accuracy with the proven methods which have won numerous National titles and have been adopted by a diverse group of champions.
Published October, 1982
Recommended for: intermediate through expert.
ISBN 0-910791-02-3 paperback

THE COMPLETE BOOK OF OPENING LEADS
by Easley Blackwood
$12.95

An impressive combination: the most famous name in bridge has compiled the most comprehensive book ever written on opening leads. Almost every situation imaginable is presented with a wealth of examples from world championship play. Learn to turn your wild guesses into intelligent thrusts at the enemy declarer by using all the available information. Chapters include when to lead long suits, dangerous opening leads, leads against slam contracts, doubling for a lead, when to lead partner's suit, and many others.
Published November, 1982.
Recommended for: beginner through advanced.
ISBN 0-910791-05-8 paperback

THE BEST OF DEVYN PRESS
Bridge Books

A collection of the world's premier bridge authors have produced, for enjoyment, this wide and impressive selection of books.

TEST YOUR PLAY AS DECLARER, VOLUME 2
by Jeff Rubens and Paul Lukacs
$5.95

Two celebrated authors ha orated on 100 challenging an tive problems which are sharpen your play. Each har sizes a different principle declarer should handle his car difficult exercises will enab profit from your errors a learning at the same time.
Published October, 1982.
Recommended for: intermedi through expert.
ISBN 0-910791-03-1 paperba

TABLE TALK
by Jude Goodwin
$5.95

This collection of cartoons i behold. What Snoopy did for Garfield did for cats, Sue and does for bridge players. If yc realistic, humorous view of and tournaments you attend brighten your day. You'll novices, experts, obnoxious alls, bridge addicts and othe ters who inhabit that fa subculture known as the brid
Recommended for: all bridge
ISBN 0-910891-04-X paperba

THE CHAMPIONSHIP BRIDGE SERIES

In-depth discussions of the mostly widely used conventions...how to play them, when to use them and how to defend against them. The solution for those costly partnership misunderstandings. Each of these pamphlets is written by one of the world's top experts. **Recommended for: beginner through advanced.**
95 ¢ each, Any 12 for $9.95, All 24 for $17.90

VOLUME I [#1-12] PUBLISHED 1980

1. Popular Conventions by Randy Baron
2. The Blackwood Convention by Easley Blackwood
3. The Stayman Convention by Paul Soloway
4. Jacoby Transfer Bids by Oswald Jacoby
5. Negative Doubles by Alvin Roth
6. Weak Two Bids by Howard Schenken
7. Defense Against Strong Club Openings by Kathy Wei
8. Killing Their No Trump by Ron Andersen
9. Splinter Bids by Andrew Bernstein
10. Michaels' Cue Bid by Mike Passell
11. The Unusual No Trump by Alvin Roth
12. Opening Leads by Robert Ewen

VOLUME II [#13-24] PUBLISHED 1981

13. More Popular Conventions b Randy Baron
14. Major Suit Raises by Oswal Jacoby
15. Swiss Team Tactics by Carol Tom Sanders
16. Match Point Tactics by Ro Andersen
17. Overcalls by Mike Lawrence
18. Balancing by Mike Lawrence
19. The Weak No Trump by Jud Radin
20. One No Trump Forcing by Ala Sontag
21. Flannery by William Flannery
22. Drury by Kerri Shuman
23. Doubles by Bobby Goldman
24. Opening Preempts by Bob Hamman

THE BEST OF DEVYN PRESS ♛

DEVYN PRESS BOOK OF BRIDGE PUZZLES #1, #2, and #3
by Alfred Sheinwold
$4.95 each

Each of the three books in this series is part of the most popular and entertaining collection of bridge problems ever written. They were originally titled "Pocket Books of Bridge Puzzles #1, #2, and #3." The 90 hands in each volume are practical and enjoyable—the kind that you attempt to solve every time you play. They also make perfect gifts for your friends, whether they are inexperienced novices or skilled masters.

Published January, 1981. Paperback

Recommended for: beginner through advanced.

⋮TS TO THE DEVIL
⋮chard Powell $5.95

⋮s the most popular
⋮e novel ever written
⋮e author of Woody
⋮'s "Bananas," "The
⋮g Philadelphians,"
⋮lvis Presley's "Fol-
⋮hat Dream."

⋮ has a cast of characters
⋮from the Kings and Queens of
⋮ent bridge down to the deuces.
⋮hem are:

⋮cKinley, famous bridge col-
⋮t who needs a big win to
⋮e his fading reputation.

⋮ Clark, who lost a husband
⋮se she led a singleton king.

⋮ Worthington, young socialite
⋮eks the rank of Life Master to
⋮ his virility.

⋮ukes and the Ashcrafts, who
⋮artnership troubles in bridge
⋮ bed.

⋮Manuto, who plays for pay,
⋮andles cards as if they were
⋮.

⋮huffles these and many other
⋮to deal out comedy, violence
⋮ma in a perfect mixture.

TICKETS TO THE DEVIL
A Novel by RICHARD POWELL
Introduction by RICHARD FREY

⋮shed 1979. . . Paperback
⋮mmended for: all bridge
⋮rs.

PARTNERSHIP DEFENSE
by Kit Woolsey
$8.95

Kit's first book is unanimously considered THE classic defensive text so that you can learn the secrets of the experts. It contains a detailed discussion of attitude, count, and suit-preference signals; leads; matchpoints; defensive conventions; protecting partner; with quizzes and a unique partnership test at the end.

Alan Truscott, Bridge Editor, New York Times: The best new book to appear in 1980 seems certain to be "Partnership Defense in Bridge."

The author has surveyed a complex and vital field that has been largely neglected in the literature of the game. The player of moderate experience is sure to benefit from the wealth of examples and problems dealing with signaling and other matters relating to cooperation in defense.

And experts who feel they have nothing more to learn neglect this book at their peril: The final test of 20 problems has been presented to some of the country's best partnerships, and non has approached a maximum score.

Bridge World Magazine: As a practical guide for tournament players, no defensive book compares with Kit Woolsey's "Partnership Defense in Bridge" which is by far the best book of its kind that we have seen. As a technical work it is superb, and any good player who does not read it will be making one of his biggest errors of bridge judgment.

The author's theme is partnership cooperation. He believes there are many more points to be won through careful play, backed by relatively complete understandings, than through spectacular coups or even through choices among sensible conventions. We agree. If you don't, you will very likely change your mind (or at least modify the strength of your opinion) after reading what Woolsey has to say.

Published 1980. . .Paperback

Recommended for: Intermediate through expert.

DO YOU KNOW YOUR PARTNER? by Andy Bernstein and Randy Baron $1.95 A fun-filled quiz to allow you to really get to know your partner. Some questions concern bridge, some don't — only you can answer and only your partner can score it. An inexpensive way to laugh yourself to a better partnership.

Published 1979   paperback

Recommended for: all bridge players.

DEVYN PRESS
151 Thierman Lane
Louisville, KY 40207
(502) 895-1354

OUTSIDE KY. CALL TOLL FREE
1-800-626-1598
**FOR VISA / MASTER CARD
ORDERS ONLY**

ORDER FORM

Number
Wanted

_____	DO YOU KNOW YOUR PARTNER?, Bernstein-Baron . . . . x $ 1.95 =	_____
_____	COMPLETE BOOK OF OPENING LEADS, Blackwood . . . . x 12.95 =	_____
_____	HAVE I GOT A STORY FOR YOU!, Eber and Freeman . . . . x 7.95 =	_____
_____	THE FLANNERY TWO DIAMOND CONVENTION, Flannery . . . . . x 7.95 =	_____
_____	TABLE TALK, Goodwin . . . . x 5.95 =	_____
_____	THE ART OF LOGICAL BIDDING, Gorski . . . . x 4.95 =	_____
_____	INDIVIDUAL CHAMPIONSHIP BRIDGE SERIES (Please specify) . x .95 =	_____
_____	BRIDGE CONVENTIONS COMPLETE, Kearse (Paperback) . . . . x 17.95 =	_____
_____	BRIDGE CONVENTIONS COMPLETE, Kearse (Hardcover) . . . . x 24.95 =	_____
_____	101 BRIDGE MAXIMS, Kelsey . . . . x 7.95 =	_____
_____	DYNAMIC DEFENSE, Lawrence . . . . x 9.95 =	_____
_____	PARTNERSHIP UNDERSTANDINGS, Lawrence . . . . x 2.95 =	_____
_____	PLAY BRIDGE WITH MIKE LAWRENCE, Lawrence . . . . x 9.95 =	_____
_____	WINNING BRIDGE INTANGIBLES, Lawrence and Hanson . . . . . . x 2.95 =	_____
_____	TICKETS TO THE DEVIL, Powell . . . . x 5.95 =	_____
_____	PLAY THESE HANDS WITH ME, Reese . . . . x 7.95 =	_____
_____	BRIDGE: THE BIDDER'S GAME, Rosenkranz . . . . x 12.95 =	_____
_____	MODERN IDEAS IN BIDDING, Rosenkranz-Truscott . . . . x 9.95 =	_____
_____	TEST YOUR PLAY AS DECLARER, VOL. 1, Rubens-Lukacs . . . . . . x 5.95 =	_____
_____	TEST YOUR PLAY AS DECLARER, VOL. 2, Rubens-Lukacs . . . . . . x 5.95 =	_____
_____	DEVYN PRESS BOOK OF BRIDGE PUZZLES #1, Sheinwold . . . . . . x 4.95 =	_____
_____	DEVYN PRESS BOOK OF BRIDGE PUZZLES #2, Sheinwold . . . . . . x 4.95 =	_____
_____	DEVYN PRESS BOOK OF BRIDGE PUZZLES, # 3, Sheinwold . . . . . . x 4.95 =	_____
_____	STANDARD PLAYS OF CARD COMBINATIONS FOR CONTRACT	
	BRIDGE, Truscott, Gordy and Gordy . . . . x 5.95 =	_____
_____	PARTNERSHIP DEFENSE, Woolsey . . . . x 8.95 =	_____
_____	MATCHPOINTS, Woolsey . . . . x 9.95 =	_____

**QUANTITY DISCOUNT
ON ABOVE ITEMS:**
10% over $25, 20% over $50

We accept checks, money
orders and VISA or MASTER
CARD. For charge card
orders, send your card number and expiration date.

SUBTOTAL [ ]

LESS QUANTITY DISCOUNT [ ]

TOTAL [ ]

_____ THE CHAMPIONSHIP BRIDGE SERIES

VOLUME 1 . . . . x $9.95 (No further discount) [ ]

_____ THE CHAMPIONSHIP BRIDGE SERIES

VOLUME II . . . . x 9.95 (No further discount) [ ]

_____ ALL 24 OF THE CHAMPIONSHIP

BRIDGE SERIES . . . . x 17.90 (No further discount) [ ]

ADD $1.00   TOTAL FOR BOOKS [ ]
SHIPPING   SHIPPING ALLOWANCE [ ]
PER ORDER   AMOUNT ENCLOSED [ ]

NAME _____

ADDRESS _____

CITY _____ STATE _____ ZIP _____